Having circled the globe 1 preaching and ministering, ... sion among church people regarding the person and the ministry of the Holy Spirit. Some refer to Him as *it*, and others are afraid of surrendering to Him lest He do things that differ from their church programs. That is why I am so grateful to Dr. Benny Tate for this great volume that explains clearly not only the person and work of the Holy Spirit but our desperate need for His daily filling. As I read this book, it ministered to me afresh, and it will do the same to you!

—Dr. Michael Youssef
Founder, The Church of The Apostles

Dr. Benny Tate has already proved he's a great leader, as the fruit of his life and ministry show. And now, in his unique and gifted way, he gives us the best insights in this book on the person of the Holy Spirit. Thank you, my friend. Every Christian needs this book!

—Dr. Bill Purvis
Pastor Emeritus, Cascade Hills Church

Pastor Benny Tate has a plain-spoken and whimsical ability to break down complex topics in a way his readers understand and appreciate. You will be blessed as Benny shares Scripture-based truths about the Holy Spirit that will deepen your faith and encourage your walk. You will greatly enjoy and be encouraged by this book.

—Rev. Will Graham,
Vice President, Billy Graham
Evangelistic Association

Pastor Benny Tate has a unique style of communication that gets to the heart of the matter. His book on the

Holy Spirit is an inspiring attempt to get Christians back to God's promises concerning the power He has made available to believers. Read it and be blessed!

—JIM CYMBALA
SENIOR PASTOR, THE BROOKLYN TABERNACLE

If ever there was a need for a book on the power of the Holy Spirit, it's today! Benny is right, "there is nothing worse than a full church of half-full people." As the world rages all around us, it's not more programs that we need. It's full churches filled with full people—people filled with the Holy Spirit. This book is a must-read for every pastor and church leader.

—JENTEZEN FRANKLIN
SENIOR PASTOR, FREE CHAPEL; *NEW YORK TIMES*
BEST-SELLING AUTHOR

UN LIMITED

BENNY TATE

WITH BRITTANY McKNEELY

CHARISMA
HOUSE

Cataloging-in-Publication Data is on file with the Library of Congress.

International Standard Book Number: 978-1-63641-267-2

E-book ISBN: 978-1-63641-268-9

23 24 25 26 27 — 9 8 7 6 5 4 3 2 1

Printed in the United States of America

Most Charisma Media products are available at special quantity discounts for bulk purchase for sales promotions, premiums, fundraising, and educational needs. For details, call us at (407) 333-0600 or visit our website at www.charismamedia.com.

To my daughter, Dr. Savannah Abigail Tate
*The Holy Spirit led your mother and me to adopt you, and it
was one of the greatest decisions of our lives. Only heaven will
reveal how proud you have made us as parents! Your mother
named you Savannah after the movie Savannah Smiles, and I
named you Abigail from the Bible because it means a father's
joy. Savannah, you have brought many smiles and much joy
to our lives!*

CONTENTS

ACKNOWLEDGMENTS

To MY WIFE, *Barbara*: Without you, there is no Benny Tate. Yes, because of your tireless and unwavering sacrifice, I have been able to live out the call on my life. Just as the Holy Spirit has been the wind beneath my wings, you have also!

To my siblings, Rhonda Armstrong, Kevin Wisdom, Vicki Steele, and Donna Wisdom: I love you all dearly and am honored to be your brother!

Jeff and Rhonda Daws: God sent you to us at a great time of need. You have been more than friends; you have been family!

Melba Williams (Mama): I love you and thank you for giving me life!

Brittany McKneely: I know there is no book without you! Thank you, more than I can express, for all you gave to make this project a reality.

Rock Springs Church family: Thank you for allowing me to be the pastor of the greatest people on earth for over three decades. The greatest joy in my life, other than my family, is being your pastor!

Rock Springs Church staff: You are the best! There is no me without we! Your teamwork has allowed the dream to work. I am honored to lead the greatest team anywhere!

Jesus Christ: You have shared Your power with me many times but never Your glory. If I have ever done any good things in my life, may You get all the praise, honor, and glory because that is where they belong!

FOREWORD

As a young mother with three small children around me twenty-four hours a day and a husband away for much of the time, I was looking for fulfillment. Anything. I volunteered. I went to parties. I was fully involved at my church. I was in Bible studies. I was organizing events. I was getting desperate.

One day a sweet friend began to talk about the Holy Spirit in a way I had not heard before. Oh, I knew about Him. I believed He was part of the Godhead. I recited the Apostles' Creed each week, which declares, "I believe in the Holy Spirit."[1] But she sounded as if she knew Him in a way that I didn't—personally, as a friend!

How could it be that I grew up in a Christian family (a rather prominent one at that), I went to Christian schools, and I even went to a Christian college, where my major was the Bible, and I still did not yet comprehend that I could know the Holy Spirt as a personal friend and guide?

Why hadn't I realized that He was more than just some nebulous Being floating around me?

Now, you would think that somewhere along the line I would have picked up enough knowledge about the Holy Spirit to know He could be known as a personal Being, a friend to me.

But I didn't. I didn't know Him the way my friend seemed to because I hadn't been taught in a way I could understand.

One afternoon I knelt beside my sofa and begged the Holy

Spirit to come into my life, to show me that He was real, that I could know Him as my friend did. Nothing changed. So the next day, I repeated my plea. Nothing changed. You see, my prayer showed my ignorance! Since I asked Jesus to be my Savior at the age of seven, the Holy Spirit was already living within me.

He wasn't the problem. I was!

I wasn't surrendering every day and every moment to Him. (Yes, it is an act of the will.) I wasn't walking with Him. Once I began the habit of breathing out my sin and breathing Him in each and every hour, I began to see His work in and through me. Now, did I do it perfectly? No, of course not—I still don't. It is, like the whole of my Christian walk, step by step, day by day.

I'll be honest with you, I don't like words such as *surrender* or *habit*. I don't like to exercise either, but I know I must to be healthy. I have learned that a healthy Christian walk requires a relationship with the Holy Spirit.

As I have gotten to know Dr. Benny Tate over the years through visiting Rock Springs Church and watching him preach online, I've realized his great heart for the Lord and people. When you hear his testimony and hear him preach, it is clear that God's hand has been on his life in a powerful way.

Dr. Benny Tate has a unique way of explaining complex ideas and concepts in a very practical way. With *Unlimited* he has given us a book to explain all that we need to understand about developing a relationship with the Holy Spirit through knowing Him personally and walking with Him moment by moment. Read it. Study it. Absorb it. Answer the questions thoughtfully. And your life will change!

—Ruth Graham
Author, *Transforming Loneliness*

INTRODUCTION
DESPERATE FOR UNLIMITED POWER

WHEN YOUR FAMILY makes a living selling whiskey illegally out of the back door of your house, there is no such thing as a good night's sleep. I can still hear that loud screeching and heavy slamming of the old screen door at the back of our cement-block house in that tiny mountain town. At all hours of the night, people were coming and going. We all took turns answering the door, taking the money, and filling the order.

Our customers were always the same people, showing up in different emotional states because alcohol affects people differently. Some were happy; others were sad. Some relaxed, while others became angry. But they all had one thing in common: wanting to drink. As long as we were selling, they were buying. We eventually got shut down, and our source of income stopped, but their drinking didn't because when a person wants to be drunk badly enough, they will find a way to get a drink every day.

God saved my life and paved a much better path than the one I lived all those years ago. I got saved at sixteen years old and have followed Jesus ever since. I can remember reading about the Holy Spirit in my Bible but having no solid understanding of Him until later in my Christian walk. You see, Ephesians 5:18 teaches, "And be not drunk with wine, wherein is excess; but be filled with the Spirit." By "Spirit" the Bible means the Holy Spirit. As a young Christian reading that scripture for the first time, I wondered why the Bible would compare being filled with the Holy Spirit with being drunk, but I later began to understand the similarities.

I know this to be true about drunk people: they will go places they wouldn't normally go, say things they don't usually say, and do things they would never otherwise do, only because they are under the influence of alcohol. If you think about it, the same is true for those filled with the Holy Spirit— they go places, say things, and do things they would never go, say, and do on their own, if it were not for the power of the Holy Spirit living inside them.

At seventeen years old, I felt called to preach, and the Holy Spirit led me into ministry. I didn't know much about the Bible. I preached out of the book of "Spasms" instead of Psalms for quite some time. There were no preachers in my family to look to or learn from. Before my mom got saved, I didn't have anyone in my life talking about church, God, or Jesus. I definitely never got to talk about the Holy Spirit. Even while attending Bible college, I didn't learn about the Holy Spirit. I couldn't remember much time or emphasis on studying or discussing the Holy Spirit in any of the classes I took.

Aside from not being taught or influenced directly concerning the Holy Spirit, there were a few reasons that I didn't try to learn more on my own. In the hills of Tennessee, where I first started preaching, the only acceptable Bible to preach from was the King James Version. Don't get me wrong, I love the King James Bible, and I preach from it to this day, but I also realize that other versions can help people understand

God's Word a little better. I believe when we get into our Bibles—whatever versions they may be—and truly seek to know God, He will provide the understanding we need at that time anyway. But early on, I would read my King James Bible and come across scripture talking about the Holy Ghost. I'll be honest, without being taught what that means, I always associated it with the only other kind of ghosts I knew about: the spooky, Halloween, campfire-story, scary-movie ghosts. To the detriment of my spiritual walk and that of others, I kept my distance from those scriptures because of my lack of knowledge.

Serving for over forty years in ministry has taught me that there is nothing worse than a full church of half-full people. I know from personal experience. My motivation for writing a book about the Holy Spirit comes from my pain. I certainly have many regrets over the last forty years of pastoring churches, but my greatest regret is neglecting to teach more about the Holy Spirit—not just because it affected me personally as the pastor but because it affected so many other people as well.

Oswald Chambers once said, "The Spirit is the first power we practically experience, but the last power we come to understand."[1] That statement is so true of my life and my Christian walk. It was the Holy Spirit that stirred in my heart as a young boy. The power of the Holy Spirit convicted my heart and led me to a moment of salvation. After knowing and serving the Lord for over forty years, I still don't completely understand the all-consuming power of the Holy Spirit, but I continue learning about Him every day.

It wasn't until 2016 that I decided to preach an entire sermon series on the Holy Spirit. I studied, prayed, and prepared more than ever before to preach for six weeks on the Holy Spirit. I didn't know exactly what to expect, but I believed the Holy Spirit would come and that great change would happen. He came indeed! And He changed everything in my personal life as well as in the lives of our church staff and congregation!

I hope reading this book leaves you believing that God wants to do the same things in your life through the power of the Holy Spirit. When you allow the Holy Spirit to fill and direct your life, everything will change: relationships will be healed, self-esteem will be lifted, purpose will be revealed, direction will become clear, hope will overflow, peace will reign in your heart, and the goodness and faithfulness of God in your life will be undeniable! If you have tried for far too long and spent too much of your valuable energy trying to manage everything going on in your life, I encourage you to surrender your strength to the indwelling presence and unlimited power of the Holy Spirit.

This book is meant to leave you with a deeper understanding of the Holy Spirit and help you realize the great importance He has in your daily life. Each section of the book is meant to provide you with a greater understanding of different aspects of the Holy Spirit working in your life. Part 1 will explain what's missing in a person's life without Christ, who the Holy Spirit really is, and why a person needs to be continually filled with the unlimited power and presence of the Holy Spirit. This section will help establish a clear foundation for the remaining chapters of the book.

In part 2 I will discuss the unlimited presence of the Holy Spirit and how His presence changes us daily to become more like Christ and helps us better fulfill the purpose He has for our lives. You will begin to see how His presence affects every aspect of who you are and how you live your life.

Part 3 will help you better understand the access you have

to the Holy Spirit's power in your life. You will gain a better understanding of spiritual warfare and the Holy Spirit's role in leading people through difficult times and claiming victory over sin. You will learn how God wants you to live when the Holy Spirit is your strength.

Part 4 will inspire you to see the Holy Spirit's presence and power in further fulfilling your purpose. This section will help you understand how the Holy Spirit teaches you, equips you, and directs you in a specific calling that God has placed on your life.

Whatever attitude or idea you have had concerning the Holy Spirit before reading this book, I pray you will be open to knowing and growing more by truly experiencing the incredible richness that comes only from maintaining a close relationship with Him! I don't want to simply provide you with textbook information about the Holy Spirit, but I hope that you can relate to, connect with, and grow from real-life, practical applications and examples provided in each chapter.

While you may not be filling up on alcohol daily like the men and women who banged on the back door of my childhood home at all hours of the night, you are filling up on something. And if it's not the Holy Spirit, you will find yourself returning to worldly sources again and again for things that will cost you so much but leave you unsatisfied. The Holy Spirit is the only satisfying source in life. The hardships and disappointments will drain you, but I'm happy to report that the Holy Spirit's power is available to you every day because His power and presence are unlimited!

PART I
YOUR UNLIMITED NEED

Don't be drunk with wine, because that will ruin your life. Instead, be filled with the Holy Spirit, singing psalms and hymns and spiritual songs among yourselves, and making music to the Lord in your hearts.

—Ephesians 5:18–19, NLT

CHAPTER 1
THE RIGHT SOURCE

I HAVE ALWAYS HATED going to the doctor. Ever since I can remember, I've avoided the doctor's office as much as possible. Now it just so happens that my doctor is a faithful member of the church I pastor; therefore, I can't avoid him for more than seven days at a time!

Prioritizing my health hasn't always been as high on my to-do list as it has been since I turned fifty years old. I've traveled all over the country preaching for over forty years, which means fast food, convenience-store snacks, sodas, and limited sleep were all a solid part of my daily routine for many years. I remember my doctor telling me during a checkup that if I didn't make some changes to my lifestyle, I wouldn't be around for many years to come. I needed to eat better, drink more water, and start exercising.

I'm proud to say I have faithfully implemented one of the three needed changes! I head to the gym at 4:30 every morning, seven days a week, to run six miles on the treadmill. If I'm traveling, the first thing I ask the hotel concierge for is directions to and information about their gym. Even on Sunday mornings I take my sermon to the gym to look over my notes while running. Some people say that if you stick with running long enough, you begin to enjoy it so much that it becomes a lifestyle.

I have a Greek word for that: hogwash. I don't enjoy running today any more than I did when I first started many years ago. Running is a necessary evil because I eat too much junk food and drink way too many Diet Mountain Dews.

My doctor and my wife, Barbara, try their hardest to get me to drink more water, but I absolutely hate it! My precious wife keeps bottled water stocked in our refrigerator at all times. But every morning, I reach right past it to grab a Diet Mountain Dew before heading to the gym.

I have been encouraged to drink at least one water for every soda I drink daily, but I'm still working on that goal. When I've tried to cut back on drinking sodas during the day, I've found myself not drinking anything at all, which can quickly lead to dehydration.

While I'm still a work in progress with making healthier choices, I do know how dangerous it can be to become dehydrated. I have learned through trial and error that staying properly hydrated is just as important as exercising daily.

According to the Mayo Clinic, "Dehydration occurs when you use or lose more fluid than you take in, and your body doesn't have enough water and other fluids to carry out its normal functions."[1] Common symptoms of dehydration include a dry mouth and tongue, weakness, a loss of appetite, and confusion. Allowing yourself to become dehydrated can be extremely dangerous to your physical, mental, and even emotional health.

Physical dehydration can be life-threatening, and if a person doesn't make the right choices to rehydrate and heal their body, death could become a real possibility. A person who begins experiencing signs of physical dehydration should be quick to seek medical attention to avoid long-term damage to the body. However, what if a person isn't dehydrated physically but spiritually?

SPIRITUALLY DEHYDRATED

I know what you're thinking: Is that even a real thing? Yes, it is! While physical dehydration means a person's body experiences a loss of water either through illness or physical activity, spiritual dehydration means a person is not being filled with living water that can only be provided through a relationship with Jesus Christ. D. L. Moody was known for praying to God to fill him with the Holy Spirit. Once he was asked why he prayed to be filled so much, and he answered, "Because I leak." If a person is not praying for a fresh filling of the Holy Spirit, they will become spiritually dehydrated.

Some people are spiritually dehydrated because they have never asked Jesus into their hearts; therefore, they have never been filled with the Holy Spirit. But don't think for a second that the only people who are spiritually dehydrated are nonbelievers, because there are Christians across the globe who are functioning in a constant state of dehydration and are attending churches that are bone-dry.

After all, Paul wrote to the saints of Ephesus, instructing them, "Don't be drunk with wine, because that will ruin your life. Instead, be filled with the Holy Spirit" (Eph. 5:18, NLT). Apparently even the church in Ephesus needed to be reminded of the importance of being continually filled with the power of the Holy Spirit.

If you compare the two conditions, spiritual dehydration has many of the same symptoms as physical dehydration. Dry mouth and tongue occur because people don't pray as they should or share the gospel with others as they are called to do. They experience weakness and give in to temptations and thought patterns that are detrimental to their overall spiritual health.

A loss of appetite occurs when people don't seek truth and

wisdom from God's Word. Confusion eventually takes over because they have become so much like the world that they cannot differentiate between truth and lies.

While both spiritual and physical dehydration can be extremely dangerous, spiritual dehydration is worse because the possibility of physical death would be a loss of what is only temporary, while spiritual death results in an eternal loss. Sadly, there are people all over the world consuming half of their body weight (number of pounds) in ounces of water daily but continually neglecting to be filled spiritually with living water.

THE PROBLEM WITH THE SOLUTION

The Bible teaches that we have a flesh problem: "For those who live according to the flesh set their minds on the things of the flesh, but those who live according to the Spirit set their minds on the things of the Spirit. For to set the mind on the flesh is death, but to set the mind on the Spirit is life and peace" (Rom. 8:5–6).

The complication, however, is that the long-term, life-altering, transformative power of the Holy Spirit is the most misunderstood solution to our flesh problem. Many people tend to disregard what they don't understand, and the Holy Spirit has certainly been disregarded by Christians and nonbelievers alike. You see, there are three groups of people in this world: those who don't know the Lord and have not received the Holy Spirit, those who know the Lord and have received the Holy Spirit but have never completely surrendered to His lordship, and those who know the Lord and are controlled by the Holy Spirit.

When considering Christianity, most people just think in terms of saved or not saved, Christian or non-Christian. Just because a person is saved and has received the Holy Spirit within them doesn't mean they have a relationship with the Holy Spirit and surrender to His powerful authority. Many Christians are living on fire insurance—they accepted Jesus to avoid going to hell. They try to make better decisions and live in a way that is pleasing to God, but they do it all in their own strength and efforts. A lot of Christians use the Bible as they would a car manual, only pulling it out to read certain sections when there is a problem. But God didn't give us the Bible simply to increase our knowledge; He gave us the Bible to change our lives.

> **God didn't give us the Bible simply to increase our knowledge; He gave us the Bible to change our lives.**

Don't be fooled: some part of every person who accepts Jesus does so to avoid hell. Our hearts are convicted of sin, and we want forgiveness so we can spend eternity in heaven. There is nothing wrong with this motivation for salvation—it's where we all begin our walk with Christ. But there comes a time when we must transition beyond being saved from hell to being saved and surrendered.

I remember desperately wanting to get saved because I was miserable from the constant thought of going to hell. As a sixteen-year-old kid, I would come home late from partying and climb into my bed, only to lie awake for hours. I knew I was living in sin, and my mother's prayers for me each night only made me feel that much worse. The Holy Spirit was dealing with my heart right up until I couldn't take it any longer, and I finally asked my mother to call the preacher. I accepted Jesus because I needed Him to get me out of hell, but it wasn't until later that I realized how much I needed Him to get hell out of me.

My salvation experience was real, and I meant every word of the prayer I prayed, but I didn't wake up the next morning free of all my bad habits and sinful behaviors. It took God one day to get the Israelites out of Egypt, but it took Him forty years to get Egypt out of them. And I had a lot of Egypt still in me. Transformation doesn't happen overnight; it is a continual process. We will all learn, grow, and develop in our walk with Christ in unique ways throughout every stage of our lives. The key is surrendering to the power of the Holy Spirit.

The problem: everyone has a tough time surrendering to what they don't understand. People who are not saved as well as Christians with no relationship with the Holy Spirit often find themselves having one or more of the following attitudes that contribute to the common disregard of the Holy Spirit: ignorance, indifference, or indulgence.

I certainly do not mean to offend anyone by using the word *ignorance*, but it simply means to be unlearned or uninformed. When it comes to the Holy Spirit, a large percentage of people are not knowledgeable and haven't been taught the truth about who the Holy Spirit is. Those who have never asked Jesus into their hearts have no true understanding of the Holy Spirit at all. To most people, Christianity is about God and Jesus: God created the world, and Jesus died on the cross. The Holy Spirit often gets talked about only as a symbol for God instead of a separate person who dwells within every Christian. First Corinthians 3:16 teaches that Christians are the temple of God and the Holy Spirit dwells within those who have accepted Christ. This concept can be quite confusing for both Christians and nonbelievers who have not been taught biblical truth concerning the Holy Spirit and His continual presence in their everyday lives.

The attitude of ignorance has kept many people from realizing the daily access they have to the presence and power of the Holy Spirit. If you currently have or have had an attitude of ignorance, it's not a reason to beat yourself up or to feel shame. I lived many years as a Christian and preached many years as a pastor with an attitude of ignorance. I didn't know the truth about the Holy Spirit, so my ignorance and fear kept me from learning for myself and sharing with others.

Learning from your mistakes is good, but learning from the mistakes of others is better. I hope you will learn from my mistakes and seek to gain a deeper understanding of the Holy Spirit through learning biblical facts provided throughout this book to help you move beyond an attitude of ignorance to discover the truth about the Holy Spirit as a person who has a mind, will, and emotions.

The second attitude concerning the Holy Spirit is one of indifference, which means a person has a lack of concern or sees something as unimportant. A large majority of people—Christians and nonbelievers alike—see the Holy Spirit as weird, strange, or mystical. He is talked about and described as a force or energy instead of being understood as a person, which causes people to see no need for understanding or even acknowledging the Holy Spirit as part of their faith.

According to the American Worldview Inventory 2021 survey conducted annually by the Cultural Research Center at Arizona Christian University, of the 69 percent of Americans who call themselves Christians, a majority (58 percent) "contend that the Holy Spirit is not a real, living being but is merely a symbol of God's power, presence, or purity."[2] There is a common feeling of indifference toward the Holy Spirit because He is more a symbol or an accessory to their faith than a vital person.

The Holy Spirit as merely a symbol of God's power and presence can be compared to the extremely popular ideas in today's culture that people can be led by their feelings of energy, vibes, and chemistry. Rather than continually being filled and led with the power of the Holy Spirit, Christians and nonbelievers alike are relying on their emotions to drive their thoughts, moods, actions, and decisions.

Relying on the flesh and working out of one's own strength is always a recipe for failure. It will always leave a person empty and dissatisfied because we were created with only one solution to our flesh problem. Saint Augustine said, "Thou hast made us for thyself, O Lord, and our heart is restless until it finds its rest in thee."[3] We must rely on a power greater than ourselves to experience peace in this life. The Holy Spirit is vital to the Christian life and should not be dismissed with an attitude of indifference.

The third attitude many people have about the Holy Spirit is one of indulgence. This attitude is developed when people have an experience that is overly excessive and not based on biblical truths concerning the Holy Spirit. Today's technology makes it so much easier for this attitude to spread because people can post and share anything on the internet that fuels misconceptions and false beliefs. It is common for someone to say something like, "I saw this crazy video online and I don't want to be a part of anything like that." While the internet can be a great tool for sharing the gospel, it is also used often to encourage sin and spread false teaching.

I know firsthand what it means to have an attitude of indulgence. Part of the reason that I avoided learning or preaching about the Holy Spirit for so long is that I had several bad experiences early in my salvation. Even before I got saved, my mother was in a relationship with a man who wasn't at all godly but talked about the Bible often. He would say things such as, "The Holy Spirit will knock you down." I can remember being extremely uncomfortable with the idea of the Holy Spirit working in my life because I didn't want Him to knock me down. I was afraid of what that meant or how that would feel.

Even after I got saved and began preaching, I remember people telling me about other church services where many in the congregation were "out of control in the Spirit." They would detail all these extreme happenings and say, "We're led by the Holy Spirit." To be honest, I was afraid. I didn't want to preach about the Holy Spirit because I feared what would happen to people and I had no idea what to expect. Because of my own fear, I stuck to the parts of the Bible I was comfortable with teaching and preaching.

Once I began deep Bible study and learned precise scripture concerning the Holy Spirit, I understood that the Holy Spirit will never violate or contradict the teaching of the Bible. I have never found any biblical basis for being "out of control in the Holy Spirit." Meanwhile, there are churches all over the world scaring people to death because they're claiming to be led by the Holy Spirit when in reality He's not within a million miles of what they are doing. Many churches today are either cemeteries (dead) or insane asylums (have crazy practices with no scriptural basis), which leaves people spiritually dehydrated and wanting nothing to do with the local church.

> **The Holy Spirit will never violate or contradict the teaching of the Bible.**

These indulgent experiences make Christians and nonbelievers hesitant to seek a relationship with the Holy Spirit. Maybe you can relate to having similar experiences and you have found yourself avoiding anything Spirit related. I encourage you to rely on scripture alone to create the foundation upon which you can build a relationship with the Holy Spirit. Don't let the actions and beliefs of others keep you from experiencing the wonderful power of the Holy Spirit working in your life. Without a fresh filling of His power daily, you will continue to feel drained and depleted. Knowing Him and surrendering to Him allows you to fully live by a power greater than yourself.

LIVING WATER

When a person is physically dehydrated, he needs to supply the body with water to replenish what has been depleted. The same is true for those who are spiritually dehydrated, but not just any kind of water will provide the necessary hydration. Living water is the only solution for spiritual dehydration.

In John 4, Jesus explains the meaning of living water while resting at a well in Samaria on his way to Galilee. As a woman approached to draw water from the well, Jesus asked that she give him a drink. She was shocked because Jews did not associate with Samaritans at that time.

He goes on to tell her, "Everyone who drinks of this water will be thirsty again, but whoever drinks of the water that I will give him will never be thirsty again. The water that I will give him will become in him a spring of water welling up to eternal life" (John 4:13–14). This woman certainly had an attitude of ignorance because she did not understand what in the world Jesus could mean by living water.

See, the woman was from Samaria, and she knew there were no rivers of "living water." The people were keenly aware of their water sources and the quality of water they had access to in the land. No doubt she was rather confused as to how Jesus could provide her with better water than she could draw from Jacob's well. But the living water Jesus refers to in this scripture is the Holy Spirit—He is the source that will never run dry for all eternity.

Jesus continues to explain in verses 23-24, "But the hour is coming, and is now here, when the true worshippers will worship the Father in spirit and truth, for the Father is seeking such people to worship him. God is spirit, and those who worship him must worship in spirit and truth." Up until this point, people worshipped God alone, but Jesus was letting her know that things were about to change greatly. True worshippers would soon worship God the Father, along with His Son, Jesus (in truth), and the Holy Spirit (in spirit).

The same is true for Christians today: we must worship God, Jesus, and the Holy Spirit. In his book *Exploring Prayer With Jack Hyles*, Hyles recalls being at a conference with John R. Rice when he opened in prayer, saying, "Oh, Father, breathe on me. Lord Jesus, help me to preach tonight. Holy Spirit, give me power." After the prayer, a young preacher questioned Rice's praying to all three members of the trinity. Rice responded, "Son, I've been in the family long enough until I know all of Them personally. I just talk to whichever One I need to talk to at the time."[4] We too must know Them personally and worship all three.

Nothing this world has to offer will ever satisfy the deepest desires of your heart and soul. Yes, this world offers plenty of temporary pleasures, but they will only leave you feeling empty after a short time. You will always be left wanting and needing more. Ecclesiastes 3:11 explains that God put eternity in man's heart; therefore, only what is eternal can provide everlasting satisfaction.

The woman at the well experienced the same longing before she came to know Jesus. For many years she had such a thirst to be loved that she sought fulfillment from men. She had been married and divorced five times and was living with a man when she met Jesus. It wasn't until she met the seventh man that her life was truly changed. Sadly, millions of people spend their lives experiencing a thirst for love, popularity, recognition, power, and other worldly things that have no eternal significance.

What had mattered to the woman at the well only moments before meeting Jesus no longer mattered, because she left her water pots to run back to town to share the news of Jesus. Those pots had been the source of life and nourishment for her body and her family, but she left them without thought because she had something greater than well water to bring back to her people.

Solomon came to the same realization in the Book of Ecclesiastes. He spent the entirety of his life seeking fulfillment through wisdom, work, wealth, wine, and women. The world's greatest pleasures and treasures were right at his fingertips, but none could satisfy his soul. He got to the end of his life and realized that the only true satisfaction a person can ever obtain comes from God alone.

I too know the disappointment that comes from seeking worldly pleasures. Before salvation, I tried just about everything to feel whole. Sports were an outlet for me, and I thought being the only freshman to make the high school team would be an achievement that brought fulfillment. When sports failed, I tried alcohol. Though I never actually liked the taste of beer or liquor, I thought it may be able to numb me into a false sense of fulfillment, as it seemed to do for so many other people I knew at the time. I partied quite a bit as well because I thought being surrounded by people would take away the loneliness I felt. Every solution I tried was as effective as putting a bandage on a bullet hole. Nothing kept me from lying in bed night after night, crying myself to sleep.

The only true solution was salvation through Jesus. Only through the power of the Holy Spirit can any person experience eternal life and peace that passes all understanding. When I knelt down by the couch in my living room and prayed the prayer of salvation, Jesus came into my life and I received the power of the Holy Spirit. How do I know the Holy Spirit came at that moment? I felt whole for the first time in my life and had joy in my heart that was not circumstantial. While nothing about my earthly situation had changed, eternity had changed for me, and my heart overflowed with a peace that I had never felt before that moment!

Maybe you are in a place of emptiness right now. Have you tried everything the world has to offer but found nothing that satisfies your soul? You may know nothing about Christianity, Jesus, or salvation. Or maybe you've spent your entire life in church on Sundays and Wednesdays just going through the motions. Acts 17:21 says, "Now all the Athenians and the foreigners who lived there would spend their time in nothing except telling or hearing something new." The Athenians were very religious, and they gathered to hear the latest teaching but didn't actually believe in one specific thing. They loved to think but never dealt in absolutes. They were the kind of people who stood firmly on both sides of every issue and were so open-minded that their brains could've rolled right out of their heads. The only problem is that we are not called to be religious. I'm not writing to encourage religion, because religion will leave you empty. True fulfillment and satisfaction will come only through salvation and seeking to know all three: God, Jesus, and the Holy Spirit.

SELF TO SAVIOR

The only solution to emptiness is turning from self to Savior. Whether you realize it or want to accept it, the Holy Spirit stirs in your emptiness and creates that longing in your heart. The emptiness will grow heavier the more He draws you to Himself. Relying on your strength, intelligence, and solutions will only drain you more and more.

Society will tell you that finding happiness, satisfaction, and contentment in life is all up to you. The popularity of relying on oneself has grown exponentially due to a self-help and self-love culture that seeks to provide all the answers to enduring life's difficulties. To be honest, that sounds like a lot of responsibility to me. While many people think being in control of their own happiness is empowering, I think it seems incredibly exhausting. Carrying the weight of this world and being your own solution to life's problems is a heavy load. There will come a time when you don't have all the answers and your best-laid plans crumble right in front of you. What then? There is no spa day, guys' night, yoga session, nature walk, or skin care routine that will heal great sorrow, disappointment, or betrayal. Sure, those things can preoccupy your mind for a short time, but they provide no long-term peace and restoration.

Another popular solution for navigating life's difficulties and achieving a brighter future is society's emphasis on good vibes and positive energy. Many people believe in the idea of creating positive energy and giving off good vibes because it will ensure happiness and contentment. The only problem with creating positive energy is that it's all up to the individuals, and when people grow weary and exhausted by all that life has thrown at them, they will need something more powerful than their own inner strength.

Good vibes are believed to create success by simply thinking, speaking, feeling, and acting positively. While I certainly believe that people should strive to maintain a positive attitude, good vibes aren't able to fix the brokenness that finds its way into all our lives at some point. Good vibes won't provide an answer for the suffering we see around the world and even within our own homes. Good vibes can't bring freedom from the shame we feel after major failure. This world is full of hurt, and good vibes just aren't enough to bring the healing we need. Should we all strive to let go of negativity? Yes. Choosing to be positive and hopeful is a wonderful attitude to have, but we aren't powerful enough to fill the emptiness in our souls.

Every person must set aside their desire to do it all through self and instead surrender to the Savior, who can bring peace, healing, and true fulfillment. If you've never asked Jesus into your heart, that's the first step. Confess your sins to Him and receive His free gift of forgiveness and eternal life. I encourage you to use the Prayer of Salvation located in the appendix to take that step to surrender your life to Christ!

You may have already asked Jesus into your heart but have yet to surrender everything to Him. You continue to live life in your own strength and struggle to maintain peace. I've got good news: let the Creator of the universe carry the heavy load because you were never meant to carry it and He has always wanted to relieve you of it!

PERCEPTION TO PRECISION

Maybe you are leery about what I'm saying because you don't quite understand or you have had experiences that have taught you differently. I encourage you to seek knowledge, ask questions, and dig deeper. Don't remain ignorant, indifferent, or indulgent concerning God, Jesus, and the Holy Spirit. Make a decision to move from perception to precision. While the Christian life requires faith, there are plenty of facts to be learned that will give you a better understanding and a firm foundation. I hope this book will be one resource that makes you more knowledgeable.

The Bible is the greatest resource you can use to move from perception to precision. Just because a pastor of a church, a speaker at a conference, or a person on the internet shared information as factual doesn't mean you have to accept it blindly. There are plenty of preachers out there sharing messages that have no biblical basis whatsoever.

Many people don't want to go to church because they've been to church. They don't want to be a Christian because they know Christians. Negative experiences in certain churches or with certain Christians only create negative perceptions about the church and Christianity as a whole.

Hypocrisy, manipulation, betrayal, and abuse have never been part of God's design for the church. All those things can occur in the church just as they can in other organizations and arenas of life because of human failure.

Christians, just like everyone else, are prone to failure and struggle with sin daily. Job 14:1 says, "Man who is born of a woman is few of days and full of trouble." Romans 3:23 says, "For all have sinned and fall short of the glory of God." Revelation 3:1–3 says, "I know your works. You have the reputation of being alive, but you are dead. Wake up, and strengthen what remains and is about to die, for I have not found your works complete in the sight of my God." The Bible is clear that even Christians will endure difficulty, fall short because of sin, and deceive others into believing they are godly. In the

Bible, God told Hosea, "My people are bent on turning away from me." Therefore, we all have a sinful nature that doesn't disappear at salvation. Instead, we have to choose every day to follow Jesus instead of our fleshly desires.

Don't rely on the behavior of others or experiences you've had to create perceptions about the Christian life. Seek to know the truth and to gain a precise understanding based on God's Word. Regardless of who says it, if something doesn't line up with the Word of God, then it's wrong. I challenge you to know God, Jesus, and the Holy Spirit with precision.

John 10:10 says, "The thief comes only to steal and kill and destroy. I came that they may have life and have it abundantly." God is not a god of little or less but the God of abundance! Look to His Word and read of His promises to those who put their hope and trust in Him. This world will leave you hopeless and empty when you try to do it all on your own, but God will fill you with Holy Spirit power and will relieve you of the burdens you carry. He offers living water that will flow into your soul and provide nourishment for all that seems dead in your life!

TIME TO REFLECT

- Which of the three attitudes—ignorance, indifference, or indulgence—seems most familiar to you? What in life has contributed to your having one or more of these attitudes?

- Jesus tells the woman at the well that she never has to thirst again. What is something that you find yourself thirsting for that only Jesus can provide?

- What do you need to surrender to God? Is it your life? Your schedule? Your loved ones?

- From what have you grown exhausted by carrying the weight in your own strength?

CHAPTER 2
THE CLOSE CONNECTION

I DIDN'T MEET MY biological father until I was thirty years old. As a child, I always wondered what it would be like to have a dad, to call someone dad, or to be called son. There was no stable father figure in my life whatsoever. I had a stepfather, but he never had a positive, much less loving, word to say to me. He always made sure everyone knew that I was his stepson when introducing me and his biological children.

As a young boy, I wanted to know what it would be like to say the word "daddy" out loud, so I would get in the corner of my closet with the door shut and say "daddy" over and over again in a quiet voice. I couldn't even picture a face while saying that word because I had never seen my father and didn't even know his true identity. Up until I was thirty years old, I believed my father to be a man named Lee Tate, but I came to find out that my real father was Don Wisdom.

I met my father for the first time at a Shoney's restaurant in Tennessee. For about an hour we made our way through introductions, pleasantries, and general information. It was awkward, to say the least. I didn't have the slightest clue as to how a meeting like that should go. Before we said our goodbyes that day, Don told me he was dying. He had lived a hard life, and his poor choices and unhealthy lifestyle had caught up to him. Thankfully, he had gone to a church service a few years back and given his life to Christ.

I wish I could say that I was able to spend the last five years of Don's life getting to know him and developing a close relationship with him, but that wasn't the case. He had a family of his own who knew nothing at all about me. In fact, I had siblings who were close in age to me because Don already had a wife and kids when he spent a few nights with my mother. He didn't want them to find out about me, so Don and I only talked over the phone, met at restaurants occasionally, and sent mail to and from his work address. I didn't meet my half-siblings until after Don passed away.

While I wasn't able to spend much time with my father those last five years, I was able to learn a good bit about him. As I got to know his personality and learned some of his mannerisms, certain aspects of my personality became clear. Don had been a professional gambler most of his life and had made a pretty good living because he was great at memorizing cards and analyzing numbers. God gave me a great memory like my father, but instead of gambling, I've been able to memorize large passages of scripture and recall names and situations rather easily. I'm also really good with numbers, which allows me to memorize dates and phone numbers. People always think it's crazy that I don't have anyone's number stored in my phone because I can remember phone numbers so easily. Being really good at remembering dates helps me remember birthdays, anniversaries, and even the specific dates when people have lost a loved one. See, God can give the same abilities to many people, but it's our responsibility to use them for His glory.

Don and I may never have developed a close relationship by any means, but I grew to know my father a little more with every conversation and every meeting. As I learned more about him, I understood more about me. I didn't get to spend a lot of time with him on earth, but I'm grateful that we get to spend eternity together!

When it comes to knowing the Holy Spirit, you have to get to know Him the same way people develop relationships. I know I'm not some super-influential person who says, "Do this," and people blindly jump on board. While we do live in a culture of social media influencers telling everyone what to wear, where to eat, the right products to buy, and the best programs to follow, my motives have never been to influence choices but to inform with truth. I don't want people to seek Jesus because it's trending or try to develop a relationship with the Holy Spirit because it's a hot topic. I want people to have a true understanding of Him in order to choose for themselves. It must be something a person willingly enters into if it's going to be a lasting decision.

For some people, that means you are learning about the Holy Spirit for the very first time because either you're not a Christian or you're new to Christianity. For others, that means you are truly learning about the Holy Spirit after years of sporadically hearing about Him in church services, Sunday school classes, and worship songs. Regardless of where you stand, I hope you will come to know the Holy Spirit instead of just knowing about Him. Reading this book won't make that happen. Sure, I can provide you with biblical truth about the Holy Spirit, which is beneficial in you making steps toward a relationship with Him. However, there must come a time when what you've learned becomes more than knowledge because you put it to the test.

REALLY KNOW HIM

When we think about knowledge, the act of knowing something usually involves information and facts, but the biblical meaning of *know* is different from our worldly understanding. Believe it or not, you can know the Bible without knowing God. In John 10:14–15, Jesus says, "I am the good shepherd. I know my own and my own know me, just as the Father knows me and I know the Father." Later, in John 17:3, Jesus prays to God, saying, "Now this is eternal life: that they know you, the only true God, and Jesus Christ, whom you have sent" (NIV). Neither of these verses talks of knowing God in the sense of having information and facts about Him.

The Greek word used for *know* in these verses is *ginōskō*, which is used to describe intimate knowledge gained through close, personal relationships.[1] *Ginōskō* is the same word used to describe the intimate relationship between a husband and wife. When a husband and wife develop a deep, intimate relationship with one another, they grow to know the other well enough to anticipate their thoughts and actions. As spouses grow in *ginōskō* knowledge, a transformation takes place in their own thoughts, actions, priorities, and values.

When you have experienced salvation through Jesus Christ, the Holy Spirit comes into your life and wants you to have *ginōskō* knowledge of Him. He longs for you to desire a deep relationship with Him so an incredible transformation can take place in your life. It won't happen overnight; as a matter of fact, it will only happen over your lifetime. Digging into the Bible is the best place to learn the truth about who He is.

FIRST THINGS FIRST

The number one thing you must understand about the Holy Spirit is that He is a person. He is the third person in the Holy Trinity. I've often heard the Trinity explained through a comparison with water. Water has three different forms—solid, liquid, and gas—but all three are still water. God is three people in one: Father, Son, and Holy Spirit. While the Holy Spirit is a person too great for us to fully comprehend, He's a person nonetheless. His incomparable greatness is often what keeps people from pursuing a lifelong journey of getting to know Him more. But how can we be more comfortable with abstract ideas such as vibes and energies than the truth of a person too mighty to be reduced to our limited understanding? It may be hard to believe that there's something too great for you to fully understand, but just because you can't believe it doesn't mean it isn't true. You can refuse to believe in having speed limits, but that won't keep you from getting pulled over!

In Genesis 1, God beautifully describes the creation of galaxies, planets, land, water, seasons, and animals, right down to humans. Genesis 1:26 explains how humans are different from any other creation because God said, "Let us make man in our image, after our likeness." Every human has a mind, a will, and emotions that make up the soul. Therefore, if humans were created in the image of God, The Holy Spirit is a person with a mind, a will, and emotions as well. He wants a relationship with you just like any relationship you may have with another person.

HIS MIND

Though we are all created in God's image, we are not all the same. God gives us unique talents, abilities, personalities, desires, and physical features. We even have an individual uniqueness in our minds. Some people are creative or abstract thinkers who enjoy new ways of doing things and making connections that others may find difficult to understand. On the other hand, some people are analytical or concrete thinkers who tend to enjoy digging into the facts using clear structures and methods, and are often practical and to the point with everything. Yes, we all have a mixture of the different ways in which the mind can work, but there is usually one way of thinking that is dominant.

My mind works mostly as an analytical and concrete thinker. I enjoy knowing the facts, and I operate with a practical thought process. I definitely like to see the end results obtained quickly and efficiently without feeling bogged down in the creative-thinking process. That's just how my mind works, and it's beneficial for those who work closely with me to know this. The Holy Spirit has a mind just like you and me, and I think it is incredibly important for us to know how His mind works. When we look at Scripture for understanding the Holy Spirit's mind, it becomes clear that His is creative.

He wants to bring transformation and renewal to every life.

If we begin at the beginning, the Holy Spirit has always been involved in creation. Genesis 1:2 says, "The earth was without form and void, and darkness was over the face of the deep. And the Spirit of God was hovering over the face of the waters." Then, again in Genesis 1:26, God said, "Let us make man in our image, after our likeness." From the creation of the world to the making of human beings, the Holy Spirit has been part of it all!

Job 26:13–14 details the Holy Spirit's creative mind when saying, "His Spirit made the heavens beautiful, and his power pierced the gliding serpent. These are just the beginning of all that he does, merely a whisper of his power" (NLT). Job was correct in saying that the Holy Spirit's involvement in creation was just the beginning and a small glimpse of what He can do.

The greatest creation in history took place in Luke 1:35: "And the angel answered her, 'The Holy Spirit will come upon you, and the power of the Most High will overshadow you; therefore the child to be born will be called holy—the Son of God.'" By the power of the Holy Spirit, Jesus' miraculous conception took place, and because of this divinely created pregnancy, we have forgiveness for our sins and the hope of eternity in heaven! I'm so thankful that the Holy Spirit's mind has always been set on creating more for us than we could ever do for ourselves!

I'm happy to report that the Holy Spirit is still in the business of creating today because His mind is set on innovating, inspiring, transforming, and renewing in the most creative ways in the lives of those who rely on Him. Psalm 104:30 describes how the Holy Spirit is who brings forth renewal in both people and nature: "When you send forth your Spirit, they are created, and you renew the face of the ground." People and places all over the world are experiencing dead and dry seasons, but when the Holy Spirit moves in a mighty way, He gives life to what is dead and nourishment to what is dry.

But He doesn't just stop with renewal. Psalm 51:10–11 says, "Create in me a clean heart, O God, and renew a right spirit within me. Cast me not away from your presence, and take not your Holy Spirit from me," which explains how the Holy Spirit is the only One who can bring transformation and truly change the human will. When the Holy Spirit comes into your life, He doesn't bring supplies to dust off your dirty heart, but instead, He creates a new heart within you.

He transforms you completely from the inside out!

The Holy Spirit's mind is set on creation, and He wants to bring transformation and renewal to every life. We are a work in progress, and we need a fresh filling of Holy Spirit power daily to bring about lasting change.

HIS WILL

The Holy Spirit also has a will—and I don't mean the kind you write up with an attorney. (That kind of will usually means trouble, because I've always found that where there is a will, there is a relative!) The type of will that I'm referring to is a person's desire, intention, and longing for certain things in life.

As humans we naturally develop a will for our own lives. There are things we desire for our lives, and we begin to make our own plans to ensure success. Most often a person's will for their life is going to be self-serving, whether through gaining power, wealth, reputation, earthly possessions, or recognition. Even if what you're doing in life helps other people, operating according to your own will is still self-serving.

Before my salvation and feeling the call to preach, I had chosen a will for my life. I had always loved watching Perry Mason as a kid, so I had plans to become a lawyer. I didn't care much about people getting saved, but I was really interested in them getting sued. I thought it would be a thrilling career to command the courtroom and argue cases as a prosecuting attorney. It turned out that God had other plans for my life. He didn't call me to defend or prosecute, only to be a witness.

The Holy Spirit has a will just as humans do, but nothing about His will is self-serving. He did not come to toot His own horn but to glorify Jesus and point people to Him. Jesus explained the Holy Spirit's will when speaking to the disciples:

> When the Spirit of truth comes, he will guide you into all the truth, for he will not speak on his own authority, but whatever he hears he will speak, and he will declare to you the things that are to come. He will glorify me, for he will take what is mine and declare it to you. All

that the Father has is mine; therefore, I said that he will
take what is mine and declare it to you.

—JOHN 16:13–15

The will of the Holy Spirit is focused solely on you knowing
Jesus and making Him known. His desire, intention, and
longing is for every person to experience salvation and become
Christlike through spiritual maturity.

For those who are saved, the will of the Holy Spirit is for
them to grow in their relationship with the Lord and fulfill
their purpose in life. John 15:26 says, "But when the Helper
comes, whom I will send to you from the Father, the Spirit
of truth, who proceeds from the Father, he will bear witness
about me." Other Bible translations replace the word "Helper"
with different descriptive names such as Advocate, Comforter,
Encourager, or Counselor. The Holy Spirit's will is to come
alongside you in your Christian walk.

In later chapters we will look specifically at the ways in
which the Holy Spirit is your helper, and we will dive deeper
into what that looks like in your everyday life. However, you
must understand that the foundation of the Holy Spirit's will
is not self-serving but Christ serving. He wants to help you,
strengthen you, give you wisdom, instruct you, and so much
more. When you make a choice to surrender your will to His
will, you can fulfill your purpose of becoming more like Jesus.

HIS EMOTIONS

What comes to mind when you think about the word *emotional*? Do you picture someone crying? If someone is described
as emotional, do you believe that to be positive or negative?
Our life experiences and home environments have a big impact
on how we think about emotions. Some people grow up in

homes where everyone shares their emotions and feels comfortable being emotional in front of other people. However, some people come from home lives that neglect to share emotions and maybe even shame others for being too emotional.

Whether you consider being emotional a good or bad thing, you were created as an emotional being. Because humans were created in the image of God, we all experience a variety of emotions over the course of our lives. The Holy Spirit also feels a variety of emotions as a divine person.

The Bible says that God is love; therefore, the Holy Spirit feels love for every one of us. In Romans 15:30, Paul writes, "Dear brothers and sisters, I urge you in the name of our Lord Jesus Christ to join in my struggle by praying to God for me. Do this because of your love for me, given to you by the Holy Spirit" (NLT). Paul points out in his letter that only by the love of the Holy Spirit can we love one another.

The same is true concerning our ability to feel hope, joy, and peace. Romans 15:13 teaches that it is only through the power of the Holy Spirt that we can overflow with hope. While there will certainly be suffering in this life, 1 Thessalonians 1:6 reminds us that the Holy Spirit gives us joy. Galatians 5:22 teaches us that, along with love and joy, the Holy Spirit produces peace in our lives regardless of our circumstances. If the Holy Spirit is to give us all these emotions, He must first have them Himself.

However, the Holy Spirit doesn't feel only positive emotions. The Bible teaches that the Holy Spirit can feel grief, anguish, and jealousy, and even be insulted. Because He loves us so much, He feels negative emotions when we choose to neglect Him or refuse Him access to our lives. Ephesians 4:30 warns us, "And do not bring sorrow to God's Holy Spirit by the way you live" (NLT). Likewise, Isaiah 63:10 tells of how our rebellion causes the Holy Spirit to feel grief. In the same way that a rebellious child can leave a parent heartbroken, our choices can do the same to the Holy Spirit.

Our neglect of the Holy Spirit can cause Him to feel jealousy as well. James 4:5 says, "He jealously longs for the spirit he has caused to dwell in us" (NIV). He wants our complete devotion to Him alone. His feelings for us are so strong that when we are weak and don't know what to pray, "the Holy Spirit prays for us with groanings that cannot be expressed in words" (Rom. 8:26, NLT). The Bible also teaches that people who treat the sacrifice of Jesus as meaningless or unimportant "have insulted and disdained the Holy Spirit who brings God's mercy to us" (Heb. 10:29, NLT).

The Holy Spirit is sensitive, and He strongly feels both positive and negative emotions. A close, intimate relationship of any kind leaves a person's emotions vulnerable. How much more must our Creator's emotions be vulnerable to His children?

IT BEGINS WITH YOUR MIND

If you are going to develop a true understanding of who the Holy Spirit is, some transformation and renewal must occur. Your mind is finite and sinful; therefore, it is impossible for you to know and understand anything holy on your own. In fact, you'll never fully know the Holy Spirit by learning through books, studies, or sermons, but by experiencing Him. It begins and ends with Him!

Paul teaches in Romans 12:2, "Do not be conformed to this world, but be transformed by the renewal of your mind, that by testing you may discern what is the will of God, what is good and acceptable and perfect." Because you were born into this world, you naturally think with a worldly mindset and are naturally driven by your flesh. However, once you've asked

Jesus into your heart, a transformation must take place for you to adopt a new way of thinking.

How do you begin thinking like the Holy Spirit? Romans 8:6 explains what you must do: "For to set the mind on the flesh is death, but to set the mind on the Spirit is life and peace." Set your mind on the Spirit. That means you must decide every day to lay down your own way of thinking and allow the Holy Spirit to guide your thinking.

The Holy Spirit is all about a new creation, not a fixer-upper. He makes all things new!

When you ask the Holy Spirit to fill you with His power and presence daily, He begins to transform your mind by creating entirely new ways in which you think about things. He's not interested in doing a little spring cleaning by tidying up your thoughts and getting rid of things that are of no use anymore. The Holy Spirit is all about a new creation, not a fixer-upper. He makes all things new!

Seeking His will for your life allows Him to bring about circumstances and experiences that will help you develop into who you were created to be! Make a choice to surrender your mind to His way of thinking so you may experience Him in a powerful way. As you lean in to the Holy Spirit and come to know Him more intimately, He will reveal to you what is holy. He doesn't want to simply increase your knowledge; He wants to transform your life so you can impact the world for Jesus!

FAN THE FLAME

Often it will be the people you know best whom you neglect or hurt the most. Why? Because you know they are more likely to forgive you. You may get so comfortable with someone that you're not as considerate of their time or how your words affect them.

The same is true for your relationship with the Holy Spirit. It can become easy to neglect Him after you've come to develop a close relationship with Him. Another word for *neglect* that is used in the Bible concerning the Holy Spirit is the word *quench*. First Thessalonians 5:19 says, "Do not quench the Spirit," which means you shouldn't do anything to prohibit Him from working in your life. There are so many amazing things He wants to do in and through your life, so you must make sure you are fanning the flame of His presence and power.

There are many things you can do in your Christian walk to fan the flame of the Holy Spirit as you get to know Him. The greatest way to fan the flame is through prayer. The Holy Spirit wants to work in every area of your life, which means continual prayer invites Him into your daily schedule.

First Thessalonians 5:17 says that you should "pray without ceasing," meaning you invite the Holy Spirit to be part of every task, every conversation, and every decision. D. L. Moody once said, "I never prayed long prayers, but I never went long without prayer." That may mean you say a quick prayer for safety while driving. For me, I say this quick prayer: "Lord, help me to say the right stuff, and nudge me when I've said enough," before going into a meeting with someone. You can know the Holy Spirit better and fan the flame of His presence in your life through prayer!

Another way to fan the flame is through gratitude. First Thessalonians 5:19 tells you to "give thanks in all circumstances," which doesn't mean you give thanks *for* everything that happens in life, but you give thanks *in* every situation.

Notice the scripture says you should give thanks, not just be thankful. You will fan the flame by expressing gratitude.

I remember, in my early days of ministry a lady in the congregation got upset with me and began to make my life miserable. She would sit through worship, but when I got up to preach, she would stand in the back and stare me down. I finally called a preacher friend of mine to tell him what was going on and ask for advice. I said, "She is making me miserable. She never has anything nice to say and always has the most hateful look on her face. What advice do you have?" My friend replied, "Thank God that you're not married to her!"

There is always a reason to give thanks. Remember, from the day of your birth to your ride in a hearse, things are never so bad that they couldn't get worse. Maybe you can't pay your bills—then just be grateful you aren't your creditors. When you develop an attitude of gratitude, you fan the flame of the Spirit in your life!

GRIEVE NOT

When a couple first start dating, they usually spend a lot of time together to get to know one another better. Both people usually begin a relationship by putting their best foot forward, and they try to avoid doing anything that would upset the other person. However, people make mistakes. The important thing to do is learn from those mistakes and do better.

A relationship with the Holy Spirit requires the same process. You aren't going to maintain a perfect relationship with Him at all times, but you can understand what upsets Him and do your best to avoid those things.

The Bible often compares the Holy Spirit to a dove, which often represents peace. All four Gospel writers chose to record

Jesus' baptism and the Holy Spirit's descending upon Him like a dove (Matt. 3; Mark 1; Luke 3; John 1). Jesus' death on the cross reconciled you back to God so peace can reign in your heart for eternity. However, you must remember this comparison to the Holy Spirit and be sensitive to Him. The Holy Spirit is sensitive like a dove, and there are things you can do to grieve Him and cause His presence to fly away.

I once heard about missionaries from Britain who were living in Israel. One day a dove nested on their roof, and they believed it to be a sign of God's blessing. However, anytime there was an argument or someone slammed the door without thought, the dove would fly away. Each time, the dove would eventually return, but the wife was always worried that one day the dove would fly away for good. She told everyone in the house that if they wanted God's blessing to remain on them, they must all adjust to the dove.

The same is true for your life—if you want the power of the Holy Spirit to remain in your life, you must be conscientious that He is sensitive. You must adjust your life in a way that cultivates an environment for the Holy Spirit to nest and not fly away. If you are like most people, adjustments need to be made to your mouth and your moods.

You can grieve the Holy Spirit with your mouth when you lie and say sinful things. Paul was very clear about how not to use your mouth: "So stop telling lies" (Eph. 4:25) and "Don't use foul or abusive language. Let everything you say be good and helpful, so that your words will be an encouragement to those who hear them" (Eph. 4:29). The words you speak are incredibly important and can have a great impact on your relationship with the Holy Spirit. There is no such thing as a little white lie. No matter the size or color, a lie is a lie. If you're not careful, what starts as one little white lie becomes one's habit of telling lies. The more you lie, the easier it becomes.

The same is true with sinful language. James, the brother of Jesus, gives this warning: "And among all the parts of the body, the tongue is a flame of fire. It is a whole world of wickedness, corrupting your entire body. It can set your whole life on fire, for it is set on fire by hell itself" (Jas. 3:6, NLT). If you're not careful with the words you speak, your mouth will grieve the Holy Spirit and cause His presence to leave.

Your moods can grieve the Holy Spirit if you are allowing anger or unforgiveness to take root in your life. Ephesians 4:26–27 tells us, "Be angry and do not sin; do not let the sun go down on your anger, and give no opportunity to the devil." When we give in to our anger, the devil takes the opportunity to create a division that allows bitterness to grow into hatred.

One morning my wife and I had an argument and got angry with each other. I remember saying, "I'm done arguing. I'll just go to church to study and prepare for Sunday." I secretly hoped that while I was gone, she would realize she was wrong and apologize to me.

I flipped pages in my Bible for hours that morning, but it got to be 3 p.m., and nothing had come of my study time. I stopped what I was doing to call home, and when she answered, I said, "Barbara, I was wrong. I love you, and I'm sorry." She apologized too, and we made things right. When I got back to studying for my sermon, it was as if scriptures were jumping off the page. Points came to my mind, and I found illustrations quickly. My sermon was prepared by the time I left for the day, and it was all because the dove had come back.

The Holy Spirit is a person with a mind, a will, and emotions, which He directs toward making God's children more like Christ. He desires closeness with you, but His incomparable greatness and holiness require you to adjust. You must set your mind on Him and be sensitive to His Spirit. Yet you cannot do these things in your own strength. Only through being filled with His power and presence can you experience the incredible transformation into the person you were created to be!

TIME TO REFLECT

- The Holy Spirit wants to bring transformation and renewal. What about your mind and thought life is in need of transformation and renewal?

- The Holy Spirit's will is Christ-centered. How can you better align your will with His in being Christ-centered today? What aspect of your life or your plans is most self-centered?

- While the Holy Spirit may be sensitive, His emotions are steady and right before God. Are you able to maintain steady emotions, or do you let circumstances impact how you feel? What emotions do you have often that are not right or pleasing to God?

CHAPTER 3
THE CONTINUAL FILLING

DURING HIS PRESIDENCY Franklin D. Roosevelt endured long receiving lines at many White House receptions. He grew tired of all the small talk and flattery he received as the host of each reception. He came to the conclusion that his guests were never really listening to anything he said while greeting and shaking hands with him. While face-to-face with the president of the United States, they seemed to have other things on their minds.

At one particular reception he decided to try a little experiment to see how attentive his guests really were. As each guest arrived and shook the president's hand, he smiled politely and said pleasantly, "I murdered my grandmother this morning."

Just as Roosevelt had suspected, the guests responded with comments such as, "Marvelous!" "Keep up the good work!" "We are proud of you!" and "God bless you, sir!"

The flattery continued almost throughout the entire line, but it was his last guest, the ambassador from Bolivia, who actually listened to what Roosevelt said in his greeting. Upon hearing the president's comment, the ambassador leaned in and whispered, "I'm sure she had it coming!"

Hundreds of guests passed right by the president without any consideration of what he was saying. They merely arrived at the reception with a rehearsed greeting and other things on their minds. Some guests may have been eager to see who else was attending the event that night. Others may have been interested in what people were wearing or what food was being served. Those with more legitimate concerns may have had their minds on an opportune conversation about politics that needed to take place during the reception. I don't claim to know exactly what the guests were thinking, but while face-to-face with the leader of the free world, they seemed to be distracted by other things.

While this story is an entertaining fact of presidential history, it also serves as an example of how Christians can miss out on being filled with the Holy Spirit. If we're not awfully careful, we will become distracted by things such as work stress, family schedules, relationship expectations, and social media platforms that keep us from experiencing the manifested presence and power of the Holy Spirit that is available to us daily. After all, the devil doesn't want to make you bad as much as he wants to make you busy. Daniel 7:25 says that he wants to "wear out the saints of the most High" (KJV).

Maybe you understand that the Holy Spirit is missing if you haven't experienced salvation. You may also understand that the Holy Spirit is a person with a mind, a will, and emotions. But you may still have important questions about what it means to be filled after salvation. Before we dive into the many reasons every Christian is in need of regular refills, let's make sure you first understand the difference between receiving the Holy Spirit and being filled with the Holy Spirit.

UNLIMITED FILLING

When a person asks Jesus into their heart and experiences salvation, they receive the Holy Spirit, who seals their salvation.

Ephesians 1:13 explains, "And now you Gentiles have also heard the truth, the Good News that God saves you. And when you believed in Christ, he identified you as his own by giving you the Holy Spirit, whom he promised long ago." When people give their lives to Christ, not only do they receive forgiveness for their sins, but they receive the Holy Spirit as a guarantee of payment and a promise of eternity. He is the seal of our salvation, reminding us that salvation is never about what we've done but what God has done!

However, the Christian life doesn't stop at salvation. It's not meant to be viewed as fire insurance to keep us out of hell. Instead, salvation must be considered the beginning of a new life. John 1:13–14 says, "But to all who did receive him, who believed in his name, he gave the right to become children of God, who were born, not of blood nor of the will of the flesh nor of the will of man, but of God." We are born again into the family of God! Therefore, salvation is a fresh departure, not a final destination.

God gives us a fresh start, but we need help to take every step in our Christian walk. God is on the throne in heaven; Jesus is seated at His right hand, interceding for us; and the Holy Spirit is who is here with us on earth. While God provided salvation through Jesus Christ, He made no provision for us to live the Christian life in our own strength. He always intended to live through us by the Holy Spirit. I'm so thankful He didn't just fix our problem and send us on our way, but He dwells within us to lead us in His way!

Ephesians 5:18 commands Christians, "Don't be drunk with wine, because that will ruin your life. Instead, be filled with the Holy Spirit." This scripture is not a suggestion but a command written to the church. The letter was meant for believers who had experienced salvation and received the Holy Spirit but were not living Spirit-filled lives.

Most Christians can read the beginning of Ephesians 5:18 and agree that it is wrong to get drunk. If a Christian walks into a church or attends their Bible study while drunk, others would certainly be in agreement that it is wrong. However, many Christians are not living Spirit-filled lives and don't give it a second thought—though the two commands are in the same verse. Just as being drunk is wrong, so is neglecting to live a Spirit-filled life.

God commands that we be filled with the Holy Spirit, but the issue with us remaining filled is that we are merely "fragile clay jars" (2 Cor. 4:7), which means we crack and leak easily. Billy Sunday once explained the only solution: "The only way to keep a broken vessel full is to keep it always under the tap."[1] Therefore, the only way to keep our leaky jars filled is by continually refilling them.

This world is an ever-changing, challenging environment that requires us to be led by the Spirit in every moment—not just in major tasks but in small reactions and decisions.

In the same way that Roosevelt's guests had access to him but didn't make the most of the time and attention they had, Christians have access to the power of the Holy Spirit but rarely acknowledge what they have been given. This world is an ever-changing, challenging environment that requires us to be led by the Spirit in every moment—not just in major tasks but in small reactions and decisions. We must acknowledge and receive the great power that is provided to us by the Holy Spirit.

I remember being at home one Saturday evening praying and talking with God about the upcoming Sunday services. I kept saying, "God, I need Your anointing for tomorrow. I need a fresh filling of Your power when I preach." I truly wanted the presence and power of the Holy Spirit to consume every part of the Sunday worship services.

Not long after I finished praying and going over my message, Barbara and I got into a conversation that led to a bit of a disagreement. We weren't fighting, but we were having some intensive fellowship when I clearly heard God say to me, "You need the Holy Spirit right now, not just when you preach." I realized at that moment that I need a fresh filling of the Holy Spirit every day so I can be the pastor I need to be as well as the husband, father, and friend I need to be. I need the power of the Holy Spirit for everything in life—and so do you!

No doubt, Christians receive all the Holy Spirit at salvation. While we can't receive more *of* Him, we can receive *from* Him more often. I am well aware that I desperately need to receive more from the Holy Spirit every day—more strength, wisdom, boldness, faith, and of every good thing He has to offer. We are all in a battle that we can't win on our own. We have a very real enemy who seeks to steal our peace, kill our hope, and destroy our lives, but we also have the weight of this world doing its very best to leave us feeling exhausted, discouraged, and empty. We all need a fresh filling of the Holy Spirit because we are certain to crack and leak under pressure. I'm so thankful that we have access to the fountain of living water who can refill us daily!

Hopefully the following chart can provide you with a clear understanding of the differences between receiving the Holy Spirit at salvation and being filled with the Holy Spirit daily

RECEIVING THE HOLY SPIRIT	BEING FILLED WITH THE HOLY SPIRIT
It happens once.	It can happen anytime.
It happens at salvation.	It happens at surrender.
It's a past event.	It's a present reality.
It's for all believers.	It's for obedient believers.
It's never commanded.	It's commanded.
It places you in the body of Christ.	It enables you to live for Christ.
It brings you into union.	It brings you into communion.
He is a resident.	He is president.
Receiving gives you pardon.	Filling gives you power.

BIBLICAL REFILLS

Being refilled or receiving a fresh filling of the Holy Spirit can be seen in Scripture through the life of Peter. On the day of Pentecost, Jesus' disciples and others were gathered together in one place when they were filled with the Holy Spirit (Acts 2:1–4). This was the first time the Holy Spirit had permanently descended upon Christians to dwell within them. He provided the seal of salvation and became a resident in their hearts. Peter, along with the others, received the Holy Spirit on Pentecost.

Later, in Acts 4, Peter and John experienced persecution for preaching the gospel and found themselves standing before the hostile high council. Acts 4:8 says, "Then Peter, filled with the Holy Spirit, said to them…," which clearly explains why Peter was able to face persecution with courage and boldly proclaim Jesus Christ. He received a fresh filling of the Holy Spirit that gave him the courage he needed and the precise words to speak at that moment.

After enduring great threats from the high council, Peter and John returned to the other believers to give a report of what had happened. They all joined together in prayer to seek God's guidance and provision. Acts 4:31 says, "After this prayer, the meeting place shook, and they were all filled with the Holy Spirit. Then they preached the word of God with boldness." This occurrence details Peter's being filled with the Holy Spirit for the third time. Each time he received a fresh filling of the Spirit, he was empowered and strengthened to continue sharing the gospel regardless of the difficulty he would face.

Just as the disciples encountered new opposition in every town they visited while sharing the gospel, we encounter new opposition and frustrating obstacles daily that drain us and leave us empty. Whether it's inconvenient interruptions, aggravating people, or unrealistic expectations, we end up pouring out until we're bone-dry. Receiving a fresh filling of Holy Spirit power each day allows us to move from exhausted to energized, fearful to faithful, divided to unified, selfish to selfless, broken to whole, and past failure to a promised future!

A powerful example of a promised future with the Holy Spirit can be seen in 1 Samuel 16, which details the anointing of David as king of Israel fifteen years before assuming the throne. In the Old Testament, the Holy Spirit came upon people for specific tasks or when a person was ordained to an official position such as kingship. Verse 13 explains, "So as David stood there among his brothers, Samuel took the flask of olive oil he had brought and anointed David with the oil. And the Spirit of the Lord came powerfully upon David from that day on." Therefore, it seems as if David had a unique experience of living with the constant presence of God in his life.

At this point in time David was a young shepherd boy who was not even close to being ready to become king, but God knew his future and began equipping him through the power of the Holy Spirit.

David would certainly need the Holy Spirit to lead and guide him as king, but even before assuming the throne, he needed the Holy Spirit with him for the everyday circumstances he would face over the next fifteen years. As David went back to his job as a shepherd, it was only through being filled with the Holy Spirit's power and presence that he was able to defend his flock against lions and bears. It was only with renewed strength from the Holy Spirit that he was able to endure ridicule from his family, defeat the Philistine giant, and flee Saul's attempts to kill him out of jealousy.

Psalm 143 is a lament from David in which he describes how exhausted and hopeless he felt because of the constant attacks and harassment from his enemies. Verse 6 says, "I lift my hands to you in prayer. I thirst for you as parched land thirsts for rain." David was empty and in need of a refill of the Holy Spirit. In verse 10 David prays, "May your gracious Spirit lead me forward on a firm footing." In his weakness he realized his need for strength and power that only comes through being filled with the Holy Spirit.

When Samuel anointed young David as king, his position had been decided, but his path had to be directed. David would face many difficult circumstances before ever wearing a crown, but the trials along the way would strengthen his relationship with God through the presence of the Holy Spirit, and he would be better equipped for kingship when the time came. The Holy Spirit came upon David and used his ordinary circumstances to equip him for an extraordinary calling!

YOUR PROMISED FUTURE

Just as David had a great calling on his life and a promised future as king, you have a great calling on your life! God has a promising future for you, and He wants to work in your life daily to direct your path. Don't get caught navigating your present frustrations in your own strength to the point of complete exhaustion. You were never meant to live the Christian life on your own. The Holy Spirit dwells within you and offers you supernatural strength to overcome life's trials. If you're not careful, you will become distracted by all that is going on around you, and you won't rely on the power within you.

> *You were never meant to live the Christian life on your own.*

God gave you the Holy Spirit to help you navigate through life; He is always with you. However, you must interact with Him to better understand where you are supposed to go and what you are supposed to do. It would be like buying a new car that has a state-of-the-art navigation system installed, but you never use it while driving. You have access to all the directions you need but will still end up lost if you don't turn it on and allow it to direct you. Just as a car's navigation system gives moment-by-moment updates on your location and prompts you at every turn, receiving a fresh filling of the Holy Spirit prepares you for specific moments throughout your day and prompts you to fulfill God's plans above your own.

DISCARD SELF

Before you begin praying, "Lord, fill me," you must first pray, "Lord, empty me." There are things in your life that have secretly taken root and now influence your thoughts, words, and actions without you knowing. Ephesians 4:22–23 instructs you to "throw off your old sinful nature and your former way of life, which is corrupted by lust and deception. Instead, let the Spirit renew your thoughts and attitudes." Before the Holy Spirit can bring renewal, you must be willing to discard the selfish, sinful things that take up space in your heart.

The emptying process will be impossible unless you rely on the Holy Spirit because you don't even know the full extent of your internal clutter. You can't just grab a pen and a legal pad to start a list of things to discard. But if you find yourself thinking that you don't know of any sin to confess, remember 1 John 1:8: "If we claim we have no sin, we are only fooling ourselves and not living in the truth." Therefore, I always encourage people to ask their close friends and family, as they're certain to point out a few things you should consider discarding! Even with the help of others, there will still be feelings, behaviors, and thoughts that only the Holy Spirit can uncover. I love what D. L. Moody said about our need to be emptied before being filled:

> I firmly believe that the moment our hearts are emptied of selfishness and ambition and self-seeking and everything that is contrary to God's law, the Holy Spirit will come and fill every corner of our hearts; but if we are full of pride and conceit, ambition and self-seeking, pleasure and the world, there is no room for the Spirit of God. I also believe that many a man is praying to God to fill him, when he is full already with something else. Before we pray that God would fill us, I believe we ought to pray that He would empty us. There must be an emptying before there can be a filling; and when the heart is turned upside down, and everything that is contrary to God is turned out, then the Spirit will come.[1]

Once you are emptied of yourself and filled with the Holy Spirit, there can be no question of who gets the glory for all the wonderful things that flow from your life. Everything good that comes from your life must be turned to praise, or it will turn to pride. God will share His generous love, provision, protection, grace, and mercy, but He will not share His glory. Allowing the Holy Spirit to empty you of anything that displeases God will ensure that you are filled with His power; therefore, you cannot accept praise for any good thing that comes from your life, because it all flows from His Spirit within you.

While you may not be able to understand and identify everything within you that is contrary to God, there is nothing about you unknown to Him. Only through divine wisdom from the Holy Spirit can you be emptied in order to be refilled completely. The decision you make to discard self and sin is not a pleasant feeling in the moment, but the fresh filling that comes from the Holy Spirit will bring peace and purpose like nothing else in the world can ever offer.

DEDICATE FULLY

If you are to experience the fullness of the Holy Spirit in your heart and life, then He must be given full control of your body, mind, and soul. At the moment of salvation, you have all of the Holy Spirit, but when you experience the filling of the Holy Spirit, He has all of you.

Surrender often means weakness, right? The world teaches that those who surrender are the ones too weak to conquer. However, the Bible teaches the exact opposite: "My grace is all you need. My power works best in weakness" (2 Cor. 12:9). When you surrender completely to God and admit that you are in need of a power greater than your own, you receive divine strength from the Holy Spirit. Why wouldn't you want to give full control to the One who loves you more than anyone, is all-wise, and is able to accomplish what's best for you?

A. W. Tozer once said, "God gives us what we want. If you want a little of His grace, you may get it. If you want to be halfhearted, you may. But if you want to be wholly His and have all His fullness, His great heart is just longing to find room and vent for His love."[2] The Holy Spirit longs for every believer to choose total surrender.

I remember going through a very low time in my early years as the pastor of Rock Springs Church. Every time we took a step forward in growing the church, there seemed to be obstacles lined up one after another. I was so discouraged and exhausted from working day in and day out to reach the community for Jesus, keep the church afloat financially, and prepare for Sunday services. When I finally reached my breaking point, I went to my office, sat at my desk, and told God that I was quitting. I remember praying, "God, I'm resigning. You are the pastor. I need the Holy Spirit to lead and direct Rock Springs Church. As of today, it's not me but You who pastors this church."

Complete dependence on God attracts the power of the Holy Spirit.

Once I removed myself from the throne and allowed God to be seated in His rightful place, amazing things began to happen in the church. Instead of relying on the presence and power of the Holy Spirit only for Sunday services, I completely surrendered every day of the week and every part of my ministry to Him. Were all our problems solved in that moment? No. But in that moment, all our problems were surrendered to the One who could solve them!

It takes humility to achieve true surrender, but complete dependence on God attracts the power of the Holy Spirit. When you dedicate yourself fully to Him, you make the life-changing decision to be wholly His and have all His fullness!

DAILY BREAD

Babe Ruth once said, "Yesterday's home runs won't win today's games." His wise words have been used over the years to motivate people to keep learning, growing, and working toward their goals because one successful milestone doesn't ensure a successful journey.

In a way, Babe Ruth's words are true for the Christian walk as well. A good Sunday sermon won't be enough to get you through the week. Matthew 6:34 teaches, "So don't worry about tomorrow, for tomorrow will bring its own worries. Today's trouble is enough for today." In the same way that you can't worry about the future, you also can't handle today's troubles with yesterday's filling.

Each new day brings an entirely new set of circumstances and experiences; therefore, you will need a fresh filling of Holy Spirit power to give you precise words, wisdom, and direction for everything you face. You will come in contact with people today whom you haven't encountered in previous days. If you commit to relying on the Holy Spirit, He will give you the right words to say in conversations and the right attitude to have in specific moments, which will allow you to share the gospel, offer encouragement, provide godly advice, and make an impact.

You need the Holy Spirit to fill you completely with everything you need for *this* day.

Moses led the children of Israel out of Egypt, and they were completely reliant on God to provide food for them in the wilderness. God was faithful to provide manna in the morning, but He was very clear that the Israelites must gather and eat only what they needed for that day, and have no to-go boxes. Exodus 16:18 says, "Those who gathered a lot had nothing left over, and those who gathered only a little had enough. Each family had just what it needed." Those who ignored God's instructions to not save any food until the next day woke up to find that the food they tried to keep was spoiled (Exod. 16:20). God required their trust in His provision alone instead of their ability to plan and prepare for days to come.

In the New Testament, Jesus taught His disciples how to pray and emphasized the very same trust God required from the Israelites. Jesus instructed them to pray, "Give us this day our daily bread" (Matt. 6:11, KJV). God is not as concerned about how much you have in life as He is about your reliance on Him to provide it all. He's not limiting you by providing you with only enough for the present day. It's quite the opposite, because when you rely on Him to provide it all, He will make sure you live out of His abundance every day of your life.

When you rely on your own ability to plan and prepare for your day, there are circumstances that you will never imagine coming your way. But living through a daily filling of the Holy Spirit's power and presence means you have divine provision for everything you face.

Sadly, preaching a funeral once every few weeks, if not weekly, has become a regular part of my schedule. No matter how many funerals I preach or how frequently they occur, each one is a special circumstance in which I need a fresh anointing of the Holy Spirit to lead and guide the service.

I can remember walking to the platform for one funeral in particular and praying, "I need Your fresh anointing." I had prepared my message in hopes of honoring the life of the deceased and comforting the family with God's Word. However, not long after I began the service, the Holy Spirit prompted me to change what I had prepared to say. He clearly said, "Stop, share the gospel, and give an invitation." I had barely begun to speak about the deceased person when He gave me very clear instructions. There was no denying that it was the Holy Spirit leading me, so I did exactly as He told me. I shared the gospel and invited anyone who didn't know Jesus as Savior to repeat after me as I prayed the prayer of salvation. As I finished praying, I asked that anyone who accepted Christ would raise their hand. Fifteen people raised their hands!

I may never have expected that funeral service to go the way it did, but I am so thankful that the Holy Spirit was leading the way instead of me. While I rejoice in that situation, I can't help but think of how many times I've missed it. How many times did I miss what the Holy Spirit wanted to do through me because I let distractions or selfish desires take the place of fresh fillings?

Make the Holy Spirit a priority every morning. Ask Him to empty you of whatever displeases God, surrender your plans to Him, and allow Him to provide a fresh filling of His power for the specific circumstances you will encounter that day. I can promise that when you choose to be continually filled by the Holy Spirit, you will live out the most exciting journey you could ever imagine! He will call you higher, take you further, and provide more abundantly than all you can ask or think!

TIME TO REFLECT

- Does the idea of being emptied completely scare you at all? Why or why not? How can your fears or hesitations keep you from experiencing the Holy Spirit moving and leading in a greater way?

- When it comes to dedicating fully, in what areas of your life do you need to resign to allow the Holy Spirit to lead? Why might it be difficult to surrender those areas?

- How might your ability to plan and prepare ahead affect your walk with the Lord? Can you plan and prepare and still trust fully? Explain.

PART II
HIS UNLIMITED PRESENCE

*But you are not controlled by your sinful
nature. You are controlled by the Spirit if
you have the Spirit of God living in you.*
—Romans 8:9, NLT

CHAPTER 4
HOMEOWNER

I HAVE OFTEN SAID that when I get to heaven, I will get to talk with all the Old Testament heroes. I imagine myself walking up to guys such as Moses, Noah, Daniel, Shadrach, Meshach, and Abednego to ask each one specific questions about what God did in their lives.

I'll ask Moses, "What was it like to stretch your rod over the Red Sea and watch that massive body of water separate to allow you and the Israelites to cross on dry ground?" I can imagine him explaining the greatness of the water as it rolled back and the awe that everyone felt at how God had moved in such a mighty way.

I'll ask Noah, "What was it like being on that boat for more than a year with all those smelly animals? How did it feel to be the only people left on earth to carry out God's plan?" I will listen intently as he explains the detailed process of building the boat and seeing all the animals arrive in pairs. He'll tell me about their daily routine of caring for themselves and the animals at sea.

Next, I'll ask Daniel, "What was it like to be in a den full of lions without getting eaten or having to fight for your life? What were those lions like all through the night?" I bet Daniel would admit to being a little fearful, and he would tell me all about the size of those lions and how he didn't sleep a wink that night.

Then, I'll ask Shadrach, Meshach, and Abednego, "What was it like to go into the fiery furnace and come out with not even the slightest smell of smoke on your clothes?" You can't even go eat at the Waffle House without that happening. I'm sure they will explain the greatness of the flames and the incredible look on the king's face when they came out of the furnace.

I imagine that after I finish asking all my questions, I will be on my way to see other things. But as I walk away, Noah will call out, "Benny, wait!" He and the others all have a question of their own to ask me.

Noah will ask, "Benny, what was it like?" I imagine myself being confused and asking him what he means. After all, I can't recall experiencing anything that compares to what they went through while on earth. What could they want to know about my life?

Moses will ask, "What was it like to have the Holy Spirit living inside of you every day? What was it like to have Him help you understand what to do moment by moment? Tell us what it was like for Him to bring scripture to your remembrance at just the right time. How did it feel to be comforted by Him when you were weak? What was it like to have the God of the universe dwell within you at all times?" I will tell them of the peace that reigned in my heart and life because of His presence. I will tell them that living with the Holy Spirit inside of me was the greatest thing I had ever experienced!

People often read about God's great miracles in the Old Testament and wish He would move in a similar way in their lives today. It's funny how hearing about someone else's great experience often makes us look at our own experiences differently. After reading about Jonah surviving in the belly of a whale, we may start to think that God hasn't done anything close to that miraculous in our lives. It might be easier to believe that God has changed His ways than to believe He is doing something even greater in His children now.

I love how Andrew Murray describes the Holy Spirit as "the best part of their birthright as God's children...the most precious gift of the Father's love in Christ—the gift of the Holy Spirit, who desires to dwell in them and lead them."[1] Murray's words explain exactly why the Old Testament saints would be curious about my experience on earth. While they were blessed to be a part of many of God's miraculous works recorded in the Bible, they don't know what it feels like to receive the most precious gift of having the God of the universe permanently dwell within them. Every Christian should be overcome with gratitude at the incredible privilege of being God's temple, but sadly, many Christians never even acknowledge His presence.

First Corinthians 3:16 says, "Don't you know that you yourselves are God's temple and that God's Spirit dwells in your midst?" (NIV). The Greek word used for *dwell* is the word *oikeō*, which means "to occupy a house."[2] The Holy Spirit wants to dwell within you permanently to speak into and lead every part of your life and every aspect of who you are. He wants a personal relationship with you and wants access to every room! He's not interested in renting space for a certain amount of time; He wants to be the homeowner with the master key in hand.

If you know anything about owning rental houses, you know it can be a bit of a hassle. You see, a lot of renters don't care about the property as much as the homeowner does. They may overlook scuffs on the wall or stains on the floor, and even allow the bushes to go uncut if they don't plan to stay for a long period of time. When renters move out, there are usually a lot of repairs needed. In some cases extensive remodeling may even need to take place.

The same is true with our bodies being the dwelling place of the Holy Spirit. If He remains the homeowner, we are taken care of with great attention, but if we let anything or anyone else rent out the space that rightfully belongs to the Holy Spirit, we'll be left broken and in need of remodeling as well.

DESPERATE WITHOUT HIM

When reading about the Israelites in the Old Testament, you may be disappointed with how quickly they turned their backs on God and forgot all He had done for them. However, you have to remember that God gave them the Ten Commandments, along with 613 other rules and regulations they had to follow with precision. Failure to meet God's standards in some cases resulted in death. God told them specifically what to do and what not to do, but it was by their own strength and ability that they had to follow the law. They didn't have the divine strength of the Holy Spirit guiding their decisions and reminding them of all that was required for them to live holy and clean before God. I can't even remember what I had for breakfast yesterday, so I'm pretty sure I would have a hard time keeping all 613 rules straight in my head.

The Holy Spirit wants to dwell within you permanently to speak into and lead every part of your life and every aspect of who you are.

The Israelites were desperate for God's guidance and were

completely lost without it. They were quick to give in to their fleshly desires because they didn't have access to a power greater than their own. They had a deep longing to be led by God, but while Moses was gone up the mountain, doubt crept into their minds. They gave in to their desperation and created idols of their own to worship. Their hasty decision to create and worship a golden calf while Moses was gone only proves that we all were created for worship, but when we get our eyes off of God and rely on our own strength, we find other people, things, or ideas to fill the void of worship.

In the Old Testament certain people experienced the Holy Spirit coming *upon* them for specific tasks or appointments, but He didn't dwell permanently *within* them. In Exodus, God gave Moses specific instructions for building His tabernacle with precision. God chose a man named Bezalel as the head craftsman, and He explained to Moses, "I have filled him with the Spirit of God, giving him great wisdom, ability, and expertise in all kinds of crafts" (Exod. 31:3). Before and after the construction of the tabernacle, Bezalel did not have the Holy Spirit leading and guiding him in whatever he did. However, God's plan for Bezalel's life allowed him access to the power and presence of the Holy Spirit while completing the tabernacle.

In Deuteronomy 34:9, Moses laid his hands on Joshua when he was selected as the one to lead the Israelites into the Promised Land. The Holy Spirit came upon him as the appointed leader. Saul and David received the Holy Spirit in 1 Samuel when they were appointed king. In Judges, the Holy Spirit came upon Othniel, Gideon, and others in order for them to serve as inspired leaders who rescued God's people from their enemies many times over.

The Old Testament saints didn't have the Holy Spirit's presence and power at all times, and He would leave once the task or appointment was completed. Very few people experienced the Holy Spirit's presence with them for the remainder of their lives. I can't imagine how awful it must feel to experience the incredible presence of the Holy Spirit in your life but then feel Him leave. I'm so thankful that I never have to know what that's like. If you have given your life to Christ, you don't have to know that terrible feeling either.

GREATNESS WITHIN YOU

The New Testament explains that the Holy Spirit doesn't temporarily come *upon* people for tasks or appointments, but He dwells permanently *within* those who have accepted Jesus Christ. Jesus told His disciples that He would soon go to be with His Father while they would remain on earth to do greater works than He. Jesus said, "I will ask the Father, and he will give you another Advocate, who will never leave you. He is the Holy Spirit, who leads into all truth. The world cannot receive him, because it isn't looking for him and doesn't recognize him. But you know him, because he lives with you now and later will be in you" (John 14:16–17, NLT). Jesus is clear that the Holy Spirit was only with them at that time but would soon live inside of them, after He ascended to heaven.

The Greek word used for "advocate" in John 14:16 is *paraklētos*, which means helper and comforter.[3] The Holy Spirit lives within every Christian and longs to provide help and comfort in all of life's circumstances.

I am reminded of the 1992 summer Olympics in Barcelona when Derek Redmond tore his hamstring while running the 400-meter race. The world watched as Derek's injury left him barely able to walk, much less able to finish running the race. He was determined to cross the finish line even if it meant excruciating pain, so he limped with tears in his eyes. To the shock of everyone watching, Derek's father ran past security guards and onto the track to help his son finish the race.[4] That moment is remembered as a beautiful example of both never giving up and a father's great love.

When the Bible uses the word "Advocate" to describe the Holy Spirit, I can't help but think of how He comes alongside us just as Mr. Redmond did for his son. God sent the Holy Spirit to live inside us because of His great love for us. The Holy Spirit wants to help us finish the race of life because we will certainly encounter circumstances that cause us to limp and feel as though we can't finish the race. We will have injuries and find ourselves in situations that require strength far greater than our own to keep going.

However, the Holy Spirit doesn't want to come alongside us only when there is a big task or when something bad happens. He wants to remain with and inside us permanently to accomplish everything in life, regardless of size or difficulty. We need Him in every aspect of our lives!

We desperately need the Holy Spirit at home. When marriage is no longer ideal but becomes an ordeal, the Holy Spirit will provide you with strength and patience to get through difficult circumstances. Parenting certainly requires the divine wisdom and guidance of the Holy Spirit, because when you are raising teenagers, you begin to understand why some animals eat their young! Parenting is tough, and it seems as if new struggles arise every day.

The Holy Spirit is vitally important in our work and social lives. When your boss or your coworkers have taken advantage of you, the power of the Holy Spirit will be the only way you will be able to treat them with love and grace. Friends will disappoint you and leave you feeling lonely, but the comfort of the Holy Spirit will remind you of how much your Father in heaven loves you!

Whether at home, at work, in social settings, or within the confines of our minds, the Holy Spirit desires to provide everything we need to honor God with our lives. Only through total surrender can the Holy Spirit lead us to fulfill our God-given purpose. He must have access to all we have and all we are. To refuse Him access to any part of ourselves or our lives will only hinder our ability to truly develop into all God has created us to be. We only endure this life by the power of the Holy Spirit, and we need Him more than we need anything or anyone else!

Ian Thomas provides a beautiful explanation of the importance of the power of the Holy Spirit living inside us, compared with us being content with a salvation experience and nothing more. Thomas said,

> To be in Christ—that is redemption; but for Christ to be in you—that is sanctification! To be in Christ—that makes you fit for heaven; but for Christ to be in you— that makes you fit for earth! To be in Christ changes your destination; but for Christ to be in you—that changes your destiny! The one makes heaven your home—the other makes this world His workshop.[5]

With the Holy Spirit permanently dwelling within every Christian, we are equipped to fulfill what Jesus said to His disciples in John 14:12: "I tell you the truth, anyone who believes in me will do the same works I have done, and even greater works, because I am going to be with the Father." The Holy Spirit equips and empowers us to spend our lives pointing the whole world to Jesus!

ALL-ACCESS PASS

Deciding to allow the Holy Spirit access to every room isn't simply a one-time decision; it's a daily practice. While you may have a moment when you decide to surrender everything to the Holy Spirit and allow Him access to every room, things will happen in life that cause certain doors to creep shut over time. If you're not careful, the Holy Spirit will become completely shut out of certain areas in your life.

When a close friend disappoints you or a relationship leaves you hurt, it's easy to let the door close rather than let the Holy Spirit have access to those circumstances. To be honest, the Holy Spirit often requires you to handle difficult situations in ways that go against your fleshly desires. Responding to hurt and disappointment with grace and forgiveness can be extremely hard when you really want to isolate or distance yourself from the ones who hurt you. But through a close relationship with the Holy Spirit and the daily practice of giving Him complete access to your life, you will experience tremendous growth in your personal life by allowing God to use your circumstances as a testimony of His goodness.

Without intentional, daily surrender, you will allow aspects of your life to become hidden or off-limits to the Holy Spirit.

The same is true for any area of your life—without intentional, daily surrender, you will allow aspects of your life to become hidden or off-limits to the Holy Spirit for a variety of reasons. No one likes to shine a light or direct attention toward the places deep within them that are vulnerable or that hold their greatest insecurities. We often want to turn a blind eye to the places that need improvement, especially when we know it requires a lot of hard work and discomfort. Don't get me wrong, we aren't capable of improving ourselves to become more like God, but disciplining ourselves to surrender to Him is hard work.

Jesus knew how hard it would be for you to live a life surrendered to God. That's why He told His disciples, "You must give up your own way, take up your cross daily, and follow me." He was clear about how often surrender must happen—daily. It's not your work that will change you or get you to heaven; it has always been through your surrender. God gives you eternity when you surrender your life to Jesus Christ, and He continues to grow and mold you every day through your decision to surrender to His way above your own. When you give the Holy Spirit complete access through daily surrender and ask Him for a fresh filling of His power, your life will become a powerful tool in God's hands! For the Holy Spirit to be a permanent resident with access to every room, you must welcome His conviction, hear His call, and seek His comfort.

WELCOME HIS CONVICTION

A person comes to the moment of salvation only by the Holy Spirit. Salvation is impossible without Him. Jesus said about the Spirit, "And when he comes, he will convict the world of its sin, and of God's righteousness, and of the coming judgment" (John 16:8, NLT).

Conviction is a role of the Holy Spirit that leads people to repentance, but conviction doesn't end after salvation. Jesus' blood paid your sin debt but didn't remove your ability to sin.

God said in Hosea 11:7 (KJV), "My people are bent to backsliding," which means you have a tendency to return to your old ways and look to your strength and plans instead of relying on His provision. When you ask God for a fresh filling of the Holy Spirit's power daily, you are choosing to surrender yourself and your day to His will and way. You must welcome His conviction above your comfort. Let Him take inventory of your heart and life every morning before you begin the day.

When you receive a fresh filling of the Holy Spirit and ask Him for a complete home inspection, you must welcome His conviction of all areas that are in need of improvement. Today, it may be your attitude that is in need of improvement. He may bring thoughts, words, or reactions to your remembrance that reveal an attitude that is displeasing to God. Tomorrow, it could be your emotions that need improvement. The Holy Spirit may convict your heart of the fear that you've let guide your emotions in certain situations. The conviction you feel may be different from day to day or it could be consistent until you have allowed the Holy Spirit to help you work through it.

Most people think of conviction as harsh or uncomfortable, but what if you chose to look at conviction through a positive lens? The Holy Spirit doesn't use conviction to prove that you're bad but to point you toward better. You see, a sinful attitude will always lead to destruction in areas such as your friendships, work ethic, and prayer life. However, welcoming conviction from the Holy Spirit will help you develop a godly attitude that will bring life to your friendships, career, and Christian walk. The same is true for your emotions. Fear will create limits to what you can do for God, but allowing the Holy Spirit to convict you of that emotion will help you trade fear for faith!

Let me hasten to say that there is a big difference between conviction and guilt or shame. Conviction comes from the Holy Spirit, while guilt and shame come from your flesh and the enemy. Jesus died on the cross so you never have to carry the burden of guilt or shame. Conviction will prompt you to repent and draw closer to God, but guilt will always prompt you to a brokenness that pushes you further from God. Understanding the distinction between the two will make all the difference in how you grow in your walk with the Lord!

Conviction isn't comfortable, but it's critical to living a life that is pleasing to God. When you close doors to different parts of yourself and refuse the transforming conviction that comes from the Holy Spirit, you may miss out on the unique plans God has for your life. He wants to mold you for a specific purpose, but you must be willing to allow all areas of your life to come under inspection and undergo a healthy transformation when necessary.

HEAR HIS CALL

If the Holy Spirit is to have access to every room in your life, you must be willing to hear His call. In the same way people screen unwanted phone calls, Christians can ignore the voice of God concerning certain topics of conversation. It's funny how easily we can make up our minds about something and convince ourselves that it's not God's voice we are hearing. Many times we think we know better than God what's best for our lives, and we become completely deaf to His voice concerning certain circumstances.

Have you ever made statements like, "God would never allow that to happen," or, "God would never tell me to go there"? You somehow already know what God would or would not do, so you refuse to hear anything relating to the "settled" areas in your life. There's just one problem: you have no way of knowing the divine plans of God. You can't begin to comprehend what He could do with your life if you truly surrendered everything to Him and agreed to be obedient to His every call.

I remember a time early in my ministry when God taught me a great lesson about hearing His call even when it seems inconvenient and uncomfortable. At the time, I would have told you that I was obedient to whatever God told me to do, but in reality, I was only obedient if His call fit my schedule. I hadn't given the Holy Spirit complete access to my time, because I thought I knew best when certain things should take place.

There had been a lady in our area who had gone to Winchester hospital and was very sick. When I was in the area, I would go by the hospital to visit her, and while I knew that she wasn't a Christian, I didn't ever talk to her about Jesus. I didn't want to make her uncomfortable. You see, I thought that a leader was supposed to keep everyone happy and please people, but I couldn't have been further from the truth. A real leader pleases God above all else. But I was young and thought I knew it all, so I avoided the subject of eternity and talked to that lady about everything else.

One Saturday morning I was making several visits on Mont Eagle Mountain when the Lord said to me, "Drop off the mountain and go see that lady." It would have been easy for me to make the visit, but I thought it was an unnecessary inconvenience at the time because I would be down there on Monday morning. Instead of obeying His call on Saturday, I rescheduled with God for Monday.

I will never forget that next Sunday morning for as long as I live. As I walked to the platform to preach, a man in the church pulled me aside to let me know that the young woman in Winchester hospital had died Saturday night. When I heard the news, my heart fell. I knew I should've gone when I had the chance. I should've shared the plan of salvation with her instead of talking about so many things that weren't eternal.

I promised God that I would never let that happen again.

I swore to let His call take priority over my schedule in the future. If He gave me another chance, I would be obedient to His call and let Him have complete access to every part of my life, not just the parts that were convenient.

When we try to decide what words from God are important, we miss the great callings in our lives and great opportunities to reach others for Jesus Christ. God's plans may not make sense to you or seem most convenient, but His plans are always perfect, timely, and necessary to fulfilling your purpose in life. I pray that you never learn to be obedient to God's call the way I did. I urge you to give Him complete access to every part of your life and commit to being obedient to His call sooner rather than later. When you follow God and leave the consequences to Him, you will avoid living with deep regret and heartbreaking guilt.

God is all-powerful, but He's also a gentleman. He gave us free will, which means all we have to do is choose. If we choose to surrender, He takes care of it all. If we choose our own way, He will remove His hand and let us try it ourselves. God didn't force my car down the mountain that day to make a visit; He let me make the decision. I learned a valuable lesson in that situation, but I learned it the hard way. Since that day, I've never regretted following His call, and He's never led me astray!

SEEK HIS COMFORT

Allowing the Holy Spirit to be your homeowner and have access to every room will require you to seek His comfort in all aspects of your life. You can't designate areas of your life as "God's comfort not necessary." While you may think certain things are too small for God to be concerned about, the truth is that God cares about everything that is a concern to you.

When your feelings are hurt over something small, God

still cares. If you don't seek His comfort in everything, you will slowly but surely turn to other things for comfort. Gradual pivots eventually lead to a 180-degree turn. Before you realize it, you will have completely changed directions and no longer seek His comfort for the big things.

You must remember that He cares about it *all*. The seemingly insignificant things that frustrate you or hurt your feelings are a concern to God because you are His child. He longs to be part of everything in your life and wants to be the One to comfort you. When you don't get invited to lunch with the others and feel left out—talk to God. When the paint didn't dry to the exact color you wanted and you're beyond frustrated—talk to God. Seeking His comfort in the little moments will prepare you to seek His comfort when the big moments arise.

If your marriage ends in divorce and you are left brokenhearted—talk to God. If you get passed up for a big promotion that you totally deserved—talk to God. In big or small circumstances, God wants to be your first Comforter. Sure, your friends, family, and spouse can comfort you in situations, but God should be your first reach. He longs to be the One you run to first, but you must give Him access to even the smallest spaces in your life.

> **God wants all of you—the good, the great, the bad, and the ugly.**

The following statement may be hard for you to accept: God wants *all* of you—the good, the great, the bad, and the ugly. There are no requirements or preexisting conditions listed in the paperwork with God. When you sell out to Him completely and allow the Holy Spirit to have access to every nook and cranny of who you are, that's when you will feel at home and at peace. You are His workmanship and His dwelling place. He longs to abide permanently within you and provide a fresh anointing on your life daily. Swing wide the doors of your heart and soul to allow the transforming power of the Holy Spirit to have complete control of your life!

TIME TO REFLECT

- Why might Christians see conviction as a harsh or negative part of a relationship with the Holy Spirit? What role do worldly standards and perspectives play in how we view conviction?

- Have you ever neglected to hear or obey God's call? If so, what were the consequences, and how did it make you feel? If not, how can you remain sensitive to His voice in every area of your life?

- What are some things in your life that are important or concerning to you but may seem too small or insignificant to be a concern for God? Have you shared your concerns with God in prayer? Why or why not?

CHAPTER 5
FROM THE INSIDE OUT

THE AMERICAN SOCIOLOGICAL Association defines *sociology* as "the study of social life, social change, and the social causes and consequences of human behavior."[1] I believe forty-plus years of ministry should earn a person a degree in sociology, because I have certainly learned a lot about human behavior while pastoring and leading people. While sociology would provide precise explanations and technical terms for certain human behaviors, the Bible provides a simple way of describing human behavior.

Matthew 7:16 is very clear about how to observe and distinguish human behavior: "You can identify them by their fruit, that is, by the way they act" (NLT). I have found this to be true with Christians. In fact, there are a variety of fruit-related classifications that apply to people within the church.

For example, there are a lot of "fruit consumers" in the average church. These people exhibit behavior that reflects they primarily take, take, take, without ever giving back. They show up wanting to know what everyone is going to do for them. Fruit consumers love the song "I Shall Not Be Moved." They will sing "Stand on the Promises," but all they really want to do is sit on the premises. When it comes to taking, these people stop at nothing.

I have also observed several "fruit inspectors" throughout my years in ministry. These delightful people analyze every detail and criticize everything that happens around the church. If they have anything positive to share, it's usually a backhanded compliment. Early in my ministry, a lady in the church was an English major. One night, after I really preached my heart out, that lady asked to speak with me. She felt the need to tell me, "Pastor, that was a good sermon, but you made thirteen grammatical errors." While I was shocked at first, I finally responded, "Sis, I had to give up 50 percent of my vocabulary when I became a Christian, so thirteen seems like a small number of errors!" I've had fruit inspectors over the years who have provided their critique of my sermons, my wardrobe, the church bulletins—you name it, and they've inspected it!

Along with the consumers and inspectors, most churches have their fair share of "fruit flies." These are the people who always gather around a stink. You know the ones I'm talking about: If there is a wayward child causing trouble, the fruit flies are gathered to hear the latest incident. When a marriage ends in divorce, the fruit flies are there to learn the cause and who is to blame. Fruit flies love to share what I like to call "gossip prayers." That's when a person says, "Now this doesn't need to spread around the church, but I think we should all be praying for Helen because she caught Harold cheating on her last night." Where there's a stinky situation, the fruit flies are sure to gather.

There have been all kinds of fruit-related people in the church over the years. I'm sure every church has them, but after pastoring for as long as I have, all these people have about made a fruit cake out of me!

THE RIGHT FRUIT

The kind of people God is looking to use within the church isn't the ones mentioned previously; He wants "fruit bearers." God longs to see His people bearing the fruit of the Spirit. I'm happy to report that I have pastored many wonderful fruit bearers throughout my years in ministry! When the Holy Spirit has complete access to your life, He begins to change you from the inside out. True life change comes only through a close relationship with the Holy Spirit. That closeness is how we develop the fruit of the Spirit permanently in our lives, and we become Christlike.

Bearing the fruit of the Spirit is not only about what we do but about who we are. When we allow the Holy Spirit's presence and power to change us from the inside out, we begin to look like Christians. Some people believe that the way to spot a Christian is by looking for those who are in their Sunday best, carrying their Bibles, bowing their heads in prayer, raising their hands in worship, and saying, "Amen," and, "God bless you." But that's not what the Bible says.

God longs to see His people bearing the fruit of the Spirit.

When the Bible speaks of Peter and John in Acts 4:13, it says the high council was amazed at them because "they could see that they were ordinary men with no special training in the Scriptures. They also recognized them as men who had been with Jesus" (NLT). When we've been with Jesus, we look different. It wasn't about how they were dressed, the religious to-do list they followed, or the eloquent language they used when quoting Scripture. It was the result of time spent with Jesus that radiated from them in everything they said and did.

I think about the story of an old farmer who began attending a very affluent church. He would go to Sunday service in his overalls and boots, while the other members wore fancy dresses and tailored suits. One day he went down front to join the church. The pastor wasn't so sure he was the right fit for their church, so he told the farmer to pray about it first. The farmer continued visiting and prayed about joining. A few weeks later he tried to join the church again, but the pastor told him to keep praying. After months of attending, trying to join, and being told to keep praying, the old farmer finally quit attending their services. When the pastor saw the farmer in town one day, he asked if the farmer quit attending because God answered his prayers. The farmer responded, "Well, I prayed about it like you suggested. And God told me that I shouldn't be upset about not being able to join because He too has tried to be a part of your church for years with no luck."

While humans often look at someone's outward appearance, God looks at what is in a person's heart. Matthew 7 explains that a good tree bears good fruit and a bad tree bears bad fruit. Verse 20 says, "Yes, just as you can identify a tree by its fruit, so you can identify people by their actions." I don't think it gets much clearer than that. Others should be able to point out Christians in a crowd not solely based on their outward appearance but because of what's on the inside. We should look, speak, and behave differently than the rest of the world.

I love what Hudson Taylor said about the noticeable change that should take place in a person's life when he or she becomes a Christian. Taylor stated:

> A candle that won't shine in one room is very unlikely to shine in another. If you don't shine at home—if your father and mother, your sister and brother, if the very

cat and dog in the house are not the better and happier
for your being a Christian, it is a question whether you
really are one.[2]

The Holy Spirit living inside a person should create an undeniable change in everything he or she says and does. When
a person maintains a close relationship with the Holy Spirit,
change begins in the heart and affects every aspect of that person's life.

In John 15:1 and 15:5 (NLT), Jesus says, "I am the true grape-
vine, and my Father is the gardener....Yes, I am the vine; you
are the branches. Those who remain in me, and I in them, will
produce much fruit." The way you are able to remain in Jesus
is through the presence of the Holy Spirit in your life. Jesus
explains the connection to the Holy Spirit in John 16:14: "He
will bring me glory by telling you whatever he receives from
me" (NLT). Therefore, you remain connected to the vine and
produce much fruit through your relationship with the Holy
Spirit.

From the moment you become a Christian, good fruit
begins to develop in your life. The fruit of the Spirit is made
up of nine attributes. When mentioned in Scripture, they are
referred to as "fruit," not "fruits," because all nine are connected to one Spirit. Therefore, you won't develop some attributes and not develop others; it's all or none.

As you continue walking in the Spirit and allowing Him to
lead you moment by moment, undeniable change will occur
in your heart and life over time. It doesn't happen all at once;
you won't wake up one morning to find that fruit has miracu-
lously ripened overnight. Instead, you will gradually begin to
experience a transformation from the inside out that affects
your countenance, conduct, and character.

AN OBVIOUS COUNTENANCE

You have unlimited access to the Holy Spirit every day. You never have to make an appointment, and He never takes a day off. Each new day brings fresh mercies and the chance to experience a fresh filling of the Holy Spirit. The internal change that begins to take place through a close relationship with the Holy Spirit begins to affect your countenance in an obvious way.

Proverbs 15:13 says, "A glad heart makes a happy face"; therefore, your countenance will noticeably change when the Holy Spirit reigns in your heart. That scripture reminds me of the little girl who looked at her grandmother across the dinner table and said, "Granny, don't be sad!" The grandmother responded, "Don't worry, sweetie. I'm not sad." The little girl said, "Oh, well, then you need to let your face know!" Your countenance speaks volumes.

Over the past twenty years of my ministry, I've had opportunities to meet with pastors from all over the country who want advice on growing their churches. They hear my story or have visited our church to see for themselves all that God has done in the little town of Milner, Georgia, and they want to know how they can experience growth and success in their churches and ministries. I try to give them practical next steps and provide as many resources as I can to help them. My team is always available to help train their staff or answer any specific ministry questions they may have. My heart has always been to help as many churches and pastors as possible. I believe that

Your countenance will noticeably change when the Holy Spirit reigns in your heart.

churches should always be about connection, not competition. We are one church!

On several occasions the pastors I have helped or advised have invited me to attend events being held at their churches. This always gives me an opportunity to get a feel for the culture of the church. Within the first ten minutes of pulling onto its campus and walking through its doors, I often know exactly why a church isn't growing. The advice I give to these churches is always the same: "Your church would grow by 10 percent if you would teach your people to smile."

It doesn't matter how great the worship sounds or how dynamic the preacher's sermon is each Sunday—if people don't feel welcome when they enter the building, they probably won't continue attending. Most first-time attendees decide whether they will return within the first ten minutes. Parking attendants, greeters, childcare volunteers, and ushers are vitally important to first impressions, and their countenance can make all the difference.

This advice applies beyond church growth to any other career field. If you run a business, people will flock to great customer service. If you manage people, the workplace environment will become healthier. If you wait tables, your tips will be better. In the world we live in, good customer service is rare. Most people expect to receive the bare minimum service from employees who are short and snappy in their interactions.

However, when someone's face lights up upon seeing you and they greet you with sincerity, you can't help but feel special. And people want to be where they feel special. Your business may not be as large as others, you may not manage as many people as other leaders, and you may not work at the fanciest restaurant, but if you create a culture of care in your own sphere of influence and have a countenance that is welcoming, people will be drawn to what you're doing and they will tell others about their great experience!

Love, joy, and peace are the first three attributes listed in Galatians 5 as the results of living a Spirit-filled life, and all three greatly affect your countenance. Romans 5:5 teaches that God gave us the Holy Spirit to fill our hearts with His love. You will begin to love people the way God loves them and find it easier to love those who haven't always shown love to you. Closeness with the Holy Spirit develops your ability to love others unconditionally because of whose they are, not who they are.

Joy is an attribute that will begin to develop inside of you through closeness with the Spirit. Joy and happiness are not the same things. Joy is an internal result, while happiness is an external result. Happiness occurs by chance and relies on what happens to you, but joy is a choice you make based on who lives within you. Proverbs 15:23 says, "A man hath joy by the answer of his mouth" (KJV), which means the words you speak are so important. You don't just need to tell yourself good things but God things. Speaking the truth of God's Word over your life will fill you with true joy!

As you grow in your relationship with God, peace will develop in your heart like never before. Philippians 4:7 says, "Then you will experience God's peace, which exceeds anything we can understand. His peace will guard your hearts and minds as you live in Christ Jesus" (NLT). When you live in Jesus through closeness with the Holy Spirit, you will experience God's incomprehensible peace in your life!

When love, joy, and peace begin developing within you, the results will be seen in your appearance. You won't be able to contain those attributes, and they will radiate on your face in everything you do. People won't be able to help but notice the difference, which will give you an opportunity to share what God's doing within you!

ORDERLY CONDUCT

A close relationship with the Holy Spirit will change not only your countenance but also your conduct. The ways in which you interact with and respond to people and circumstances will begin to reflect Jesus more and more as the Spirit continues to develop patience, kindness, and goodness within you.

Patience that develops from closeness with the Holy Spirit means that you are far from anger. Impatient behaviors are a result of selfish motives, and when things don't go your way or happen within your time frame, impatience can produce anger rather quickly.

I remember as a boy I could lose my temper rather quickly, but my mom would always help me find it! As I've gotten older, I've learned how to control my temper better, but I'm not perfect. When my daughter, Savannah Abigail, was little, she would ride with me in the car to different places. One day while riding with her mother, she asked, "Mama, how come when Daddy drives, all the idiots come out?" I must admit that the Holy Spirit has been developing patience within me for many years. We all have different attributes that may take more time to develop than others, and mine is patience!

Surrendering completely to the Holy Spirit means you no longer operate in your own strength or schedule. If you acknowledge that everything in your life is from God and allow Him to determine your every step, you will develop greater patience because you know that nothing is yours to control in the first place. You will be more careful with the words you speak because you understand that "the tongue can bring death or life" (Prov. 18:21, NLT). Divine patience will always lead you to choose life!

Closeness with the Holy Spirit will also help you develop kindness, which this world is so desperate for now. Ephesians 4:32 instructs us to "be kind to each other, tenderhearted, forgiving one another, just as God through Christ has forgiven you" (NLT). Kindness in today's world seems like a rare attribute to witness. Instead of compassion and forgiveness, many people want to see others called out, humiliated, and condemned for all they've done wrong. It seems as if people are looking for the bad in others instead of the good.

I am aware that there are people all over the world who aren't looking for the bad in others, but many times they aren't looking for anything at all because they're so busy. Busyness is the enemy of kindness. People get so caught up in their own circumstances that they don't make time for a nice compliment or smile while waiting in line for coffee. When heads are down and eyes are glued to phone screens, not a kind word or gesture will be spoken. However, if the Holy Spirit instead of your schedule leads your day, you will become more sensitive to His promptings and better recognize opportunities to share kindness with those around you.

If you acknowledge that everything in your life is from God and allow Him to determine your every step, you will develop greater patience because you know that nothing is yours to control in the first place.

Your conduct will also change concerning goodness in your heart when you seek closeness with the Holy Spirit daily.

Abraham Lincoln once said, "Whatever you are, be a good one."[3] He was talking about a person's values. The word used for "goodness" in Galatians 5:22 is *agathōsynē*, which means "uprightness of heart and life."[4] As the Holy Spirit develops goodness in your life, you will be more concerned about what is right over what is popular.

An opinion is something you hold, but a conviction is something that holds you. When you ask the Holy Spirit for a fresh filling and follow His lead, you will be driven by your divine convictions instead of your fleshly opinions. Many decisions in life are hard to make, but they are so much harder when you don't know what your values are.

When you walk in the Spirit daily, goodness can be seen in everything you do. You will be led by godly convictions that result in others having confidence in who you are as a person. Your conduct will be orderly and right in the eyes of God through a close relationship with the Holy Spirit.

OBEDIENT CHARACTER

As closeness with the Holy Spirit results in a great transformation of your countenance and conduct, you will also observe change within your character as you develop faithfulness, gentleness, and self-control. Here's what I know: if you will take care of your character, God will take care of your reputation. Your character is developed and strengthened through a close relationship with the Holy Spirit.

Walking in the Spirit daily will produce faithfulness in your heart and life. Revelation 2:10 promises that when you remain faithful even in the face of death, you will receive the crown of life. Faithfulness is the character of someone who can be relied on. This means day in and day out, a person is obedient to God's commands and the leading of the Holy Spirit.

God used certain people in the Bible because of their faithfulness. God chose to use David to defeat the giant because he had been faithful to feed the sheep. First Timothy 1:12 says, "I thank him who has given me strength, Christ Jesus our Lord, because he judged me faithful, appointing me to his service." Many times we think, "If I could just get the position, I would be faithful," but that's not biblical. Scripture teaches that God considers a person faithful before giving them a position.

The same is true concerning faithfulness in your relationships with others. When I pastored a little church in Tennessee many years ago, there was a businessman in our church who was experiencing great success with his business expanding. He had three daughters who were a little concerned because the nature of the business's success meant that their daddy would be working with a lot of other women. They went to their mother and said, "Mama, we're not really sure about Daddy doing business with these women. You just need to keep your eyes on him." Their mother said, "Girls, I'm not worried about him." The girls explained, "But Mama, you don't know these women." Then the mother explained, "I may not know those women, but I know your daddy."

When you walk closely with the Holy Spirit, people will consider you faithful and a person of good character. People will look to you as a leader because you have a track record for always doing what's right in God's eyes.

As you strengthen your character concerning faithfulness, you will also begin to develop gentleness. Another word used in different translations of Scripture is "meekness." Many times people associate meekness with weakness, but in reality, meekness is best described as power under control.

There are four hundred leaders mentioned in the Bible, but only eighty of them were described as finishing faithfully. If you study the 20 percent who finished faithfully, you will find they all had one thing in common: humility. All the great leaders are humble. Jesus is the greatest leader to ever live, and the only description He ever gave of Himself was in Matthew 11:29: "I am humble and gentle at heart" (NLT). If you are to become more like Jesus, then you must allow the Holy Spirit to work within you to develop meekness.

The last fruit of the Spirit mentioned in Galatians 5:23 is self-control. A true indication of the Holy Spirit working in your life should be self-control because your character will exhibit restraint over your fleshly desires. No doubt, you will face battles concerning a desire for things such as recognition, appetite, lust, and revenge, but the Holy Spirit will develop self-control in your life that allows you to overcome temptation and maintain an obedient character. When you want to respond to someone's hateful comment, you will pray for them instead. Although it feels good to receive attention and compliments from the opposite sex, you will avoid tempting situations and seek God's approval above all else. You will allow the Holy Spirit to guide your life so you won't do what your sinful nature desires (Gal. 5:16).

As Christians we're called to be different. Instead of looking like the world, we should resemble Jesus in all that we say and do, but we can't do it in our own strength. There isn't one person on earth with enough willpower to endure an attack from the enemy or the temptations of the flesh. It is only by the power of the Holy Spirit living and working inside of us that we can become more like Jesus. It's a transformation that happens from the inside out.

THE VINE IS THE SOURCE

If you are going to truly experience the power of the Holy Spirit developing fruit in your life, you must commit to doing three things: connecting, pruning, and remaining.

Connecting to the vine is the beginning of fruit production in your spiritual life. You can't produce anything lasting and valuable until you are connected to the vine. Connecting makes fruit. The Holy Spirit enters your heart and immediately begins working to transform your heart. Only through connecting to Jesus through salvation can you have a relationship with God. According to John 15, Jesus explained that He is the vine, we are the branches, but God owns the vineyard. Everything belongs to Him!

Jesus explained the importance of our connection, but He went on to explain how our relationship with Him grows and develops over time. Once we are connected and begin to produce fruit, pruning must take place. Jesus said that God "prunes the branches that do bear fruit so they will produce even more" (John 15:2, NLT). Connecting makes fruit, but pruning multiplies fruit. God is the God of abundance, and He always wants more for you. Pruning only takes place because God wants you to bear even more fruit in your life.

Think of it like parenting—children must learn the discipline to grow and mature into healthy adults. Of course, no child enjoys being disciplined by their parents, but it teaches them many necessary and healthy lessons about life. Pruning brings discomfort in the moment but will multiply the fruit that is produced over time.

You are certain to face difficulties in life, but look at every obstacle as an opportunity for growth. Challenging situations that test your values may come at work or in your relationships, but you will have an opportunity to stand firm in truth and glorify God with your choices. You will most likely encounter people who push your buttons every chance they get, but you will have the opportunity to exhibit patience and self-control. You may experience wilderness seasons where you feel all alone, but choose to see them as opportunities to remain joyful and not let your circumstances steal your peace.

I can remember a time in my ministry when three of the closest people in my life and my ministry were no longer working alongside me. In a year's time each of those people moved out of my ministry to follow the Lord in serving at other churches and even in other states. God used that season of pruning to teach me to rely on Him alone.

As our church had grown, I relied on those three people for support, encouragement, and advice for navigating all the new growth we were experiencing and the decisions that we were facing. When God led them elsewhere, I was left to rely only on the wisdom and support of the Holy Spirit. He had to be the first person I consulted in my decision-making, and I had to seek encouragement from God's Word. While it was an incredibly difficult time in my life, I'm so thankful that God used that season to strengthen my relationship with Him and to continue developing me into the preacher and leader He wanted me to become.

Once you have connected to the vine and started making fruit, you must endure the moments of pruning so that fruit can be multiplied in your life. When others see you exhibiting the fruit of the Spirit while enduring the painful, frustrating, and challenging moments in life, you sow seeds for the Holy Spirit to move in their hearts. Your life becomes a testimony of God's goodness!

Yes, God wants you to connect to the vine to make fruit

and endure the pruning to multiply fruit, but He always wants more for you. Jesus went even further in John 15:5 to explain, "Those who remain in me, and I in them, will produce much fruit" (NLT). Apparently you can go beyond producing *more* fruit and begin producing *much* fruit.

Remaining in Jesus will maximize fruit in your life. How can you remain in Jesus? Through a close relationship with the Holy Spirit. What does that look like? Being consciously aware of the Holy Spirit's presence in every moment of your day.

Every time you say yes to God and allow pruning to take place, He removes the weeds that hinder growth. He will remove the worldly burdens that try to weigh you down. He will increase your ability to impact others for Him. He will enlarge your coast and equip you for more. When you remain in Him every morning and hide His Word in your heart, you can maximize every moment for eternity. The Holy Spirit will prompt you to speak life and love into someone at just the right moment. The peace you maintain will be felt in every room you enter. The kindness you show will encourage others who are struggling with insecurities.

> **Every time you say yes to God and allow pruning to take place, He removes the weeds that hinder growth.**

You see, when the Holy Spirit transforms your life from the inside out, you can't help but spill the fruit of the Spirit onto everyone you encounter. It becomes who you are and what you do without even trying. When you focus on the Father, you can't help but produce fruit. But if you ever try to focus on the fruit and produce in your own strength, things will quickly turn from ripe to rotten. There is no fruit without Him!

I pray that you won't settle for simply making fruit when

you can live a life that multiplies and maximizes the fruit of the Spirit. When you allow the Holy Spirit to transform you from the inside out, your fruitful life will impact others for eternity.

TIME TO REFLECT

- Which of the nine attributes of the fruit of the Spirit seems to be the most difficult to develop in your life? Why?

- Why is it so difficult for Christians to endure the pruning seasons while also remaining close with God? How do worldly relationships impact this aspect of our spiritual lives?

- How can your choice to remain in Jesus maximize fruit in your life? Who could be or needs to be impacted by your choice to remain in Jesus and bear the fruit of the Spirit?

CHAPTER 6
CHOOSING WISELY

AT TWENTY-FIVE YEARS old I made one of the biggest decisions of my life. I didn't realize it at the time, but that one decision would shape my entire life and ministry forever. Twenty-five years old—I was just a kid. I've never understood why we end up making some of the most important decisions of our lives before we ever have the chance to really live and gain experience. Most people choose a career, get married, and even have children before the age of thirty. Looking back now, I'm not sure I knew anything at all before the age of thirty.

I may not have understood the magnitude of the decision I was making, but in 1990 Barbara and I made the choice to leave our church, our families, and everything familiar to us to move to Georgia. We had always lived close to our families. I was a full-time pastor at a little church that had grown to around three hundred people, and we were being recognized by the denomination for being the fastest-growing church in our area. We loved the little town we lived in at the time more than anywhere else we'd ever lived. It made no sense to anyone for us to leave. Well, it made no sense to anyone but God!

While I thought it would be a neat opportunity to preach a

weekend revival at Rock Springs Church in Milner, Georgia, God thought it would be *the* opportunity to radically change my life and the lives of so many others. He had more than a revival in mind!

God knew I loved pastoring the little church in Tennessee and that I wouldn't be open to leaving, so He chose to speak through Barbara. I often say that husbands who don't listen to their wives miss 50 percent of what God's trying to tell them. After I had preached the Friday night service and got into our vehicle to leave, Barbara said, "Benny, I think we're supposed to come here." I was quick to say, "No, I don't think so. We're not supposed to come here." I remember thinking, "Who leaves a church of three hundred to pastor a church of thirty?"

I preached on Saturday night and again on Sunday morning to close out the revival, and I'll never forget the feeling I had when I got into my Dodge pickup truck to head home. I made it to the end of Rock Springs Road and stopped. I started crying and put my head on the steering wheel. I told Barbara, "I'm willing to come. I don't want to come here, but I believe it's the Lord's will."

After pastoring Rock Springs Church for over thirty years, I can say it is one of the greatest decisions I've ever made. The church with thirty members turned into a church with thousands in attendance every Sunday. The one chapel turned into multiple campuses. The one Sunday service turned into three service times in person and online. Our family of two turned into three with the adoption of our daughter, Savannah Abigail. God spoke to me during that 1990 revival, and I made a decision because I heard from Him. I chose His will over my own, and His plans for my life far exceeded anything I could have planned for myself!

Here's what I've learned: we often make choices, and then our choices make us.

Decisions determine our destiny, but we don't have to decide on our own or live with the constant stress of indecision. Two things are true about decisions in life: we will constantly be faced with them, and God wants to help you make the right ones! But here is the key question: Are you asking for His help and listening for His answer?

THE HOLY SPIRIT SPEAKS

John 16:13 (NLT) says, "When the Spirit of truth comes, he will guide you into all truth. He will not speak on his own but will tell you what he has heard. He will tell you about the future," which means the Holy Spirit, the One who is here with us, wants to guide our lives and give direction to our decision-making. He is always willing to speak into our situations, but we have to ask for His guidance and be able to recognize His answers.

Asking God to help us make the right decisions is the easy part, but we may struggle to hear His answers, especially if we don't know how He will communicate with us. If we want to hear the Holy Spirit speak, we must maintain closeness with Him and understand that He communicates in a variety of ways. Let's take a look at five ways the Holy Spirit communicates.

One of the ways in which the Holy Spirit will speak to us is through God's Word. It is so important that we not only read the Bible but hide it in our hearts so we might remember it at just the right time. I'm reminded of the pastor who got invited to his friend's house for lunch but couldn't get him to answer the door. He sent the following text: "Look! I stand at the door and knock. If you hear my voice and open the door, I will come in, and we will share a meal together as friends." A few minutes later his friend sent this reply: "I heard the sound of you in the garden, and I was afraid, because I was naked, and I hid myself." Knowing God's Word will surely be useful in the right circumstances!

Psalm 119:105 (NLT) says, "Your word is a lamp to guide my feet and a light for my path," which means the Bible gives us direction and helps lead us down the right path in life. The answer for every-thing we need can be found in God's Word. John 14:26 says this about the Holy Spirit: "He will teach you all things and bring to your remembrance all that I have said to you"—but keep in mind that He can't bring something to our *remembrance* that we haven't first read and studied. Therefore, it is vitally important that we are reading and studying God's Word daily so we can hear from Him first concerning how we should live and which choices we should make. So often we are listening for a voice instead of looking for a verse.

> **If we want to hear the Holy Spirit speak, we must maintain closeness with Him and understand that He communicates in a variety of ways.**

Before Barbara and I began dating and got married, I would pray for my future wife. I wanted to marry the woman God had for me, but I never opened my Bible and found a scripture that specifically said, "Benny Tate, you will marry Barbara Roberts." However, the Bible was very clear about the type of woman I should marry and what a godly marriage should look like.

Scripture taught me that I shouldn't be "unequally yoked"

(2 Cor. 6:14) but that I must find a wife who loves God more than she loves me. Proverbs 31 taught me to seek a wife who is trustworthy, generous, wise, supportive, and encouraging, and who makes sure her home and her family are built on a godly foundation. I relied on God's Word to provide the right criteria for choosing a wife instead of what the world said was the right criteria. God's Word has never failed in leading me in the right direction, and He certainly blessed me with the best wife!

Another way the Holy Spirit communicates with us is through gut feelings. What separates humans from animals is not our minds, wills, or emotions, but our spirits. When we accept Jesus Christ at salvation, our spirits are awakened and connects with the Holy Spirit. Many people refer to the feelings they have as gut feelings when their conscience tells them certain things. Romans 9:1 (NLT) explains this feeling: "With Christ as my witness, I speak with utter truthfulness. My conscience and the Holy Spirit confirm it." When we have true gut feelings, it is the Holy Spirit communicating to our consciences.

I have known people who made decisions that no one else seemed to understand, but they told me, "I just know it is God's plan." There have also been times when I have personally had the gut feeling to walk away from certain situations or avoid going to certain places. I remember Barbara having a similar gut feeling when I was pastoring Sweeten Hill Church in Tennessee, but I made the mistake of not listening to her. Several people in the church had made plans to go to the Lake Winnepesaukah theme park on a Saturday, but Barbara said she didn't think we should go. I was hard-headed and told her we *would* go to the theme park after I got off work because I thought we would have a lot of fun!

Remember when I said that husbands miss 50 percent of what God tries to say when they don't listen to their wives?

That was certainly true in this situation. When Saturday came, Barbara said, "Benny, I just don't think we're supposed to go. I have a bad feeling about it." I ignored her concerns about going. Right when we were turning into the entrance of the theme park, a big truck came through the intersection and hit our little truck on Barbara's side. We were hit so hard that our vehicle went off the side of the road and was completely totaled. When I got control of the truck and it came to a stop, I looked over at Barbara and said, "Baby, are you OK? Are you OK?" She said, "Yes, Benny, I'm OK. I'm fine. But I told you we weren't supposed to come today." I believe God tried to keep us from that accident by communicating with Barbara through a gut feeling, but I was too stubborn to listen. I have certainly learned my lesson and am attentive to both my and Barbara's gut feelings.

God may not audibly tell you which job offer to choose, but He can give you a gut feeling about a potential employer or work environment. While He gives characteristics of godly husbands and wives in Scripture, He doesn't specifically name the person you should marry. But He can give you that gut feeling of just knowing a certain person is the one for you. The more you develop a close relationship with the Holy Spirit, the more you recognize and trust His direction.

Peace is another way the Holy Spirit communicates concerning our decision-making. Colossians 3:15 says to "let the peace that comes from Christ rule in your hearts." The word "rule" used in this scripture means "to act as an umpire."[1] If something is God's will for your life, peace will lead the decision. I often use the word *peace* as an acronym in determining if something is God's will.

P—providential: Did I open the door, or did God open the door? Did it fall in my lap?

E—enemy: What would the enemy want me to do? Do the opposite.

A—authority: Does this decision align with God's Word? Is it biblical?

C—confidence: Does confidence build in my heart with this decision?

E—ease: Am I at ease and do I have peace in my heart as I make the decision?

An example of using the acronym to determine God's will happened with a man I once knew who had received two big job opportunities. One opportunity led to a good career that would allow him to not only provide for his family but spend more time with them. The other opportunity was a considerable promotion to a very prestigious position. Before knowing about his job offers, I knew that he had been having some trouble at home and that he and his wife were going through a difficult time in their marriage. Most of the letters in the acronym would be easy for him to answer, but when he came to me for advice, I asked him about the E—which job would the enemy want you to take? He quickly identified the job that would take time away from his family. He knew that the considerable time apart from his wife and children was not worth the increase in salary. The enemy would want him to choose to have more money over having a healthy marriage. He allowed the Holy Spirit to guide his decision-making and was able to choose the job that brought peace to his heart and life.

The Holy Spirit wants to do the same for us. While we may be nervous about certain decisions, especially the big life decisions that require us to take one step at a time without seeing the bigger picture, we can still have peace in our hearts that we are being obedient to what God is calling us to do and making the decision He would have us make!

Visions and dreams are another way the Holy Spirit communicates with us. In Acts 2:17, God says, "I will pour out my Spirit upon all people. Your sons and daughters will prophesy. Your young men will see visions, and your old men will dream dreams" (NLT). The Holy Spirit speaks to us by putting a vision in our hearts. Helen Keller was once asked if she thought there was anything worse than being blind. She responded, "The only thing worse than being blind is having sight and no vision." God gives us great visions because He has much that He wants to accomplish through us for His glory!

God gives us vivid dreams as well. We all dream every night, whether we remember or not. In fact, the National Sleep Foundation says most people dream for about two hours each night, but "dreams can be forgotten in the blink of an eye."[2] Though most dreams escape our memory, a dream from God stays with us. I believe He shows us things in our dreams because it bypasses our rational thinking. We often limit ourselves based on what we understand about our current circumstances, but God sees what we can be and what our futures hold. Many times we dismiss a big idea as too lofty of a dream before we have given the Holy Spirit time to move or work in our circumstances.

When Barbara and I were going through the adoption process, I had a vivid dream one night that stuck with me after I woke up. We finally got a call that we were chosen to adopt a little baby that would be born within a few short months. As Barbara and I prepared our home, I remember her asking me what I thought the baby would be. I told her that God had shown me in a dream that we would have a little redheaded girl. Our baby was born, and the adoption agency called us to let us know she was a girl and she had strands of red hair. We knew instantly that she was the one!

I believe God knew the difficulties we would go through concerning our adoption process. We had been allowed to see our baby girl right after she was born but found out later that we couldn't go back to visit because the mother wasn't sure if she would go through with the adoption. Of course, we were upset, but I clung to what God had shown me in that dream, and I knew it would all work out for us to adopt that little red-headed girl. And to this day, Savannah Abigail has been the love and light of our lives! God used a dream to communicate His direction for our lives and to give us peace in difficult circumstances.

Philippians 2:13 (NLT) says, "For God is working in you, giving you the desire and the power to do what pleases him"; therefore, the great visions and dreams that are big in your heart are God-given desires that are meant to lead you in the direction you were created to go in and accomplish all the things you were created to do for God! Things will always be big in your heart before they are big anywhere else. The Holy Spirit will speak to you through visions and dreams to help you make the right decisions for your life. Be sure you aren't limiting what He can say or how He can say it by dismissing a vision or dream.

The Holy Spirit uses people to communicate with us concerning decisions we should make. David said in 2 Samuel 23:2, "The Spirit of the LORD speaks through me; his words are upon my tongue," which means the Holy Spirit can give specific words to people to help guide others in their decision-making. Matthew 10:19–20 is clear about how the Holy Spirit speaks through us and others in a timely way: "God will give you the right words at the right time. For it is not you who will be speaking—it will be the Spirit of your Father speaking through you." God spoke through the disciples in biblical times, and He continues to speak through His people today!

I remember a time in my ministry when I was exhausted. I had been going too much and was burning the candle at both ends. A good friend and mentor in my life, Dr. Richard Lee, called me one day and said he needed to come down to see me in person. He had no idea how exhausted I had become. When he arrived at my church, he took one look at me and said, "Benny, let's go outside. I need to say something to you." We walked outside where we could be alone, and he looked me straight in the eyes and said, "For everything you're saying yes to, you're saying no to something else. You don't realize it, but you're saying no to your wife, daughter, health, and private time with God." I knew immediately that God had sent Dr. Lee to my church to give me that message.

You see, I have the propensity to say yes because I truly want to do whatever I can to help people. I have always had a really hard time saying no, even when I believe it's the right thing to do. Helping people is my heart, and I wish I could say yes to everything that is asked of me, but God used Dr. Lee to teach me a valuable lesson that day. He spoke directly through Dr. Lee to help me realize the root of my exhaustion. Over the years, I have been intentional about having mentors in my life who pray for me and speak truth into my life, and I have also been intentional about praying for others and allowing God to use me to speak into the lives of those around me as well.

> *Surrounding ourselves with godly people is incredibly important because God will often use others to point us in the right direction and speak truth into our circumstances at just the right time.*

Surrounding ourselves with godly people is incredibly important because God will often use others to point us in the right direction and speak truth into our circumstances at just the right time. Attending church regularly, getting involved in a life group, and having a godly mentor are vital connections and relationships that contribute to our spiritual growth. It is such a blessing to have people who will pray for you and seek God on your behalf concerning important decisions and circumstances in your life, but you should also strive to be that person in someone else's life.

PREPARED TO HEAR

I have found that many people do not have a hard time believing that God sent His Son to die on a cross, but a lot of people have trouble believing that He loves us enough to send us a message. Throughout my years in ministry I've heard people make statements such as, "I don't think the Holy Spirit speaks to me," "I don't think God is going to tell me what to do in this situation," or "The Holy Spirit doesn't care about my little problems." If you find yourself thinking these things about your own life, let me remind you of what 2 Corinthians 13:14 says: "May the grace of the Lord Jesus Christ, the love of God, and the fellowship of the Holy Spirit be with you all" (NLT).

As a believer you have been given grace through Jesus Christ, you are loved unconditionally by God, and the Holy Spirit longs to fellowship with you! *Merriam-Webster* defines *fellowship* as "a friendly relationship" and "a sharing of interest or feeling."[3] Therefore, the Holy Spirit longs to speak to you because that's what friends do. He cares about everything that interests or concerns you. So it's not a matter of *if* the Holy Spirit speaks to you but *when* and *how* He speaks.

When we adopted Savannah Abigail, the agency gave us medical information concerning her biological parents. We learned that her biological father was deaf, so we paid close attention to Savannah's hearing as she got older. When she was around three years old, Barbara and I noticed that Savannah wasn't responding to our voices consistently. I would call her from across the room, but she wouldn't look in my direction. Barbara and I began to worry that she may be losing her hearing, so we took her to the doctor immediately.

Once the doctor did a full exam, he informed us that she had a significant amount of wax buildup inside her ear that was hindering her ability to hear clearly. After a quick procedure to remove the excess wax, I said, "Savannah?" She immediately said, "Daddy!" While she thought we hadn't been speaking to her much, the truth was that she just couldn't hear us.

The same can be true in our relationship with the Holy Spirit. We would like to believe that He isn't speaking, but the majority of the time, we just aren't prepared to hear Him. We have our own blockages that hinder our spiritual ears. Doubt, disobedience, and distractions are three common reasons we aren't hearing the Holy Spirit speak in our lives.

DOUBTING HE WILL

When it comes to trusting the Holy Spirit to speak, I think we can be like the guy who slipped over the edge of a cliff and was holding on to a little tree branch. He yelled out, "Help me, God!" A moment later, God said, "Do you believe in me?" The man responded, "Yes, I do!" God then asked, "Do you trust me?" The man responded again, "Yes, I do! I trust you!" God finally said, "Then let go of the branch." The man quickly asked, "Is there anyone else up there I can talk to?"

Hebrews 11:6 says, "Anyone who wants to come to him must believe that God exists and that he rewards those who sincerely seek him" (NLT). I am convinced that the reason many people don't experience the Holy Spirit speaking to them is that they don't truly believe He will speak. Many people spend their lives believing in God and His great love for them in sending His Son as payment for their sin debt. They don't doubt God's existence or their salvation in Jesus, but they doubt that the Holy Spirit will speak directly into their lives concerning their decisions and circumstances.

To overcome doubt and hear from the Holy Spirit, you must first decide in your heart that you believe He will speak to you. Doubt is a part of everyone's faith journey; we all battle it at some point. James 1:5 says, "If you need wisdom, ask our generous God, and he will give it to you. He will not rebuke you for asking." God is not mad or disappointed when we have doubts, but He does want us to use that opportunity to seek Him for wisdom and guidance. Commit in your heart to seek closeness with the Holy Spirit and expect Him to speak to you.

You must also commit to believing what you hear instead of writing it off as a coincidence. If you're not sure if something is from God, ask Him for clarity and see if it aligns with the Bible. Just because you don't fully understand it doesn't mean it isn't the Holy Spirit speaking. Dig into God's Word and seek Him through prayer for greater clarity.

The Holy Spirit may speak to you through a friend who randomly texts you an encouraging scripture when you're having a bad day. You may show up to Bible study and learn that the lesson applies precisely to what you're going through. You may be getting ready for work one morning and have an overwhelming feeling to check in on your friend. None of these things are coincidences. Regardless of how unexpected the situations seem, choose to believe that God can speak to you in many different ways throughout your day. It's amazing how often you will hear from the Holy Spirit when you are expecting Him to speak. You can prepare to hear Him better by eliminating doubt and choosing to focus your attention on Him in expectation!

DISOBEYING HIS WORDS

I once had a man tell me, "God doesn't speak to me anymore." I wasn't sure what he meant, so I asked, "Did God used to speak to you?" He answered, "Yes." Curiously, I asked, "Did you obey Him when He spoke?" The man said, "No." I couldn't help but respond, "Then why would He keep speaking?"

Disobedience is a reason that many Christians don't hear from the Holy Spirit. In Mark 4:24–25, Jesus said, "Pay close attention to what you hear. The closer you listen, the more understanding you will be given.... But for those who are not listening, even what little understanding they have will be taken away from them." Just as Jesus taught His disciples in biblical times, the Holy Spirit teaches and leads us now, but we have to be obedient in listening to what He says. If you ask the Holy Spirit for direction but refuse to follow where He leads, why should He continue speaking when He knows that you won't accept His direction or instruction?

You must get to a place of total

If you ask the Holy Spirit for direction but refuse to follow where He leads, why should He continue speaking when He knows that you won't accept His direction or instruction?

surrender and choose complete obedience if you want the Holy Spirit to direct your daily life. We may never fully know the impact our obedience may have on our lives and the lives of others. In the same regard, we may never know the impact of our disobedience.

The Holy Spirit already knows your answer to His directions and instructions long before He asks. Remember, He sees your heart full of all its motives and intentions. Why would He continue asking you to do something when He knows your heart is set on disobedience? The longer you are disobedient, the more distant you will grow in your relationship with the Holy Spirit. He wants to guide you in every decision you make, but you must commit to following His lead regardless of your own plans or reservations. You will never regret being obedient to what the Holy Spirit calls you to do!

DISTRACTED BY THE WORLD

I believe the biggest reason people don't hear the Holy Spirit speaking in their lives is because of distractions. The Holy Spirit will most likely speak to you in a still, small voice that can't be heard unless you are close and quiet. In 1 Kings 19, Elijah wanted to hear from the Lord. He stood waiting as a strong wind, an earthquake, and a fire occurred, but the Lord was not in any of those things. When he finally heard the Lord, it was a gentle whisper.

In order to hear the Holy Spirit speaking, you have to eliminate the distractions of this world. That means you might have to cut a few things from your schedule to make time to get alone with God. You will have to put down your phone and quiet your notifications. You are in this world in contact but you're not meant to be in the world in conduct; therefore, your pace and your priorities will look different from most people's. If the devil can't make you bad, he'll try to make you busy. It is easy to become so distracted by all that is going on in the world that you can't hear the Holy Spirit speaking.

You will have to quiet other voices in your life as well to better hear from the Holy Spirit and make the right choices. The voices you listen to will determine the decisions you make, and so many times people are running to the phone instead of the throne. If you're not careful, you will talk to everyone else about your circumstances and the decisions you need to make instead of talking to God and creating an environment in which the Holy Spirit can clearly speak to you.

The Holy Spirit wants to be in close communication with you every day and longs to give you direction in every decision you face, but you have to desire the same closeness and attention to Him. If you will follow the Holy Spirit and seek closeness with Him, you will always make the right decisions. I know it has been true for my life that every time I have leaned on the Holy Spirit to guide my decisions, I've made the right choice. However, every time I've leaned on my own strength and understanding, I've regretted not letting the Holy Spirit guide me.

Maybe you need to start believing that the Holy Spirit cares deeply for you and will speak to you daily. You may have heard from God in the past but must decide in your heart to be obedient to whatever He asks you to do now. If your life is full of distractions, you may need to silence the noise and revise your schedule to better hear the Holy Spirit speak. Whatever your circumstances may be, I know that the Holy Spirit wants to speak to you. He is faithful to direct you in every decision you face if you will trust Him above all else!

TIME TO REFLECT

- Chapter 6 detailed five different ways the Holy Spirit can speak. Is there one way in which He's spoken to you more than the others? Which way do you prefer most when hearing from the Holy Spirit?

- Have you ever disobeyed something that you know the Holy Spirit told you to do? If so, how did you feel when you were disobedient? What type of circumstances do you think cause most people to be disobedient?

- What is the biggest distraction in your life that keeps you from hearing the Holy Spirit clearly? What changes can you make this week to limit distractions and better hear the Holy Spirit speak?

PART III

HIS UNLIMITED POWER

But you will receive power when the Holy Spirit comes upon you. And you will be my witnesses, telling people about me every-where—in Jerusalem, throughout Judea, in Samaria, and to the ends of the earth.

—ACTS 1:8, NLT

CHAPTER 7
THE STRONGEST DEFENSE

OVER THE YEARS, I've had several opportunities to speak to the students at Columbia International University in South Carolina. One day the president of the university, a good friend of mine, called me to say he appreciated my willingness to come speak every time he'd asked and said he wanted to do something for me to show his gratitude. He proceeded to tell me he was going to take me on a bear hunt!

Let me be clear, I'm not a hunter. I have never really understood why anyone would want to get out of a warm bed to climb into a cold tree. But my friend said he was going to take me to northern Maine, just shy of the Canadian border, to hunt a bear, so I figured I would go for the unique experience.

After getting all the information from him about the trip, I started thinking more about encountering a bear up close. I got in bed that night and began thinking of how I would be in a tree stand by myself in the dark. I became scared as my mind ran wild with the possibility of a bear coming up the tree while I was in the stand. No one around me for miles. Just me and a bear. Needless to say, I didn't get much sleep.

I woke up the next morning with a plan to get myself prepared for the hunt and avoid any dangerous encounters in a tree stand. My first phone call was to a man in our church who is an avid big-game hunter. I told him about the hunting trip I was going on and asked him for his advice because I had no hunting gear, no gun, and absolutely no knowledge of how to shoot a bear if I did end up seeing one. The man invited me to his house and said he would make sure I had everything I needed!

Because he knew I was pretty nervous about the hunt, the man chose a specific gun to shoot and said, "This gun can kill any size animal in North America." I was already feeling better! He then took me to the gun range to practice shooting. Every time I shot the target, I asked, "Would that shot kill a bear?" With each good shot, I felt more and more at ease.

As I left the range, I asked the man if I could take the gun home. He said, "Well, I don't really think you need to be shooting it where you live!" I said, "No, I'm not going to shoot the gun. I just want to familiarize myself with it. I want to hold it, get the scope zeroed in, practice loading and unloading it, and know everything I can about this gun." He agreed to let me take it home. Each night I would spend time getting used to the feel of the gun and how it operates. I would look through the scope to make sure I could see clearly and aim accurately. I made sure I knew every inch of that gun. Then, I would go back to the range and practice shooting. I did this regularly until it was time for the hunt.

When it came time to pack for the trip, I asked the man if I could use that exact gun for the hunt. I didn't want to use the guns they would have for me in Maine. I wanted to use the one that I felt so confident with because I knew it so well. He agreed to let me take it. When I arrived in Maine, the guys leading the hunt said, "Before we take you out in the woods by yourself and leave you twenty feet in the air, we need to see you shoot the targets." I got my gun loaded and positioned myself to shoot. Bam! I shot the target and hit the bull's-eye. One guy said, "The preacher can shoot!" By the time they put me in that tree stand, I was ready to see a bear, because I felt like Dirty Harry, "Go ahead, make my day!"

The very same guy who had been so afraid just a few months before the trip was now confident in taking down a bear. What made the difference? The weapon. I had familiarized myself with the weapon and felt confident in its ability to protect me since I knew how to use it properly. I knew the capability and power of that weapon, which meant I was capable and powerful in protecting myself because I knew how to use it.

DAILY ATTACKS

While the average person is not preparing for a bear hunt, I know for sure that we are all fighting battles every single day. We may not have to worry about a bear attack, but we have an enemy who attacks us every day. Ephesians 6:11–12 (NLT) explains,

> Put on all of God's armor so that you will be able to stand firm against all strategies of the devil. For we are not fighting against flesh-and-blood enemies, but against evil rulers and authorities of the unseen world, against mighty powers in this dark world, and against evil spirits in the heavenly places.

There is a spiritual battle going on around us every day whether we choose to acknowledge it or not. We have a very real enemy who wants to destroy our lives and leave us hopeless. He will wait patiently for just the right time to attack. That's why 1 Peter 5:8 says, "Stay alert! Watch out for your great enemy, the devil. He prowls around like a roaring lion, looking for someone to devour" (NLT). Our enemy is very real, and if we want to be prepared for battle, we must be familiar with our greatest weapon, our strongest defense—the Holy Spirit.

Jesus told His disciples that they would receive power when the Holy Spirit came upon them (Acts 1:8), and the same is true for you and me. When people experience salvation, not only do they receive forgiveness and the promise of eternity, but the Holy Spirit dwells within them and gives them a divine power that's stronger than anything in the world. Zechariah 4:6–7 teaches, "It is not by force nor by strength, but by my Spirit, says the LORD of Heaven's Armies. Nothing, not even a mighty mountain, will stand in Zerubbabel's way; it will become a level plain before him!" (NLT). You see, no strength or force of our own can defeat the devil, but if you have the Holy Spirit living inside of you, His strength can turn a mountain into a level plain in an instant!

We must make preparing for battle a priority in our everyday lives.

If anyone intends to win a battle, they have to know two things: who their enemy is and what their strategy for defense is. In the same way an army wouldn't run into battle completely blind with no knowledge of their enemy, we cannot live our lives completely unaware or unconcerned about our enemy, who prowls around us like a lion, just looking for an opportunity to completely devour us. We must make preparing for battle a priority in our everyday lives.

STEP 1: ENEMY ANALYSIS

First, know your enemy and his strategies. In John 10:10, Jesus describes the devil as a thief when saying, "The thief's purpose is to steal and kill and destroy. My purpose is to give them a rich and satisfying life" (NLT). We have an enemy who doesn't just want to make us bad or knock us off our game, but he wants to completely destroy our lives and keep lost people from experiencing salvation through Jesus Christ.

Theft by Deception

Jesus said the devil comes to steal, but what exactly does he want to steal? He wants to steal peace by attacking the mind to create confusion and doubt. The devil has no new tricks or schemes; he continues to use the very same method today that he's used since creation.

Genesis 3:1 shows the devil's desire to create doubt in Eve's mind when he said, "Did God really say you must not eat the fruit from any of the trees in the garden?" Then again, in verses 4–5, he said, "You won't die!...God knows that your eyes will be opened as soon as you eat it, and you will be like God, knowing both good and evil."

The devil began with confusion by distorting the truth. Notice how the wording of his first question creates confusion by causing Eve to wonder if she had heard God clearly—did He *really* say that you can't eat from *any* of the trees? The devil always wants us to doubt whether we are hearing God correctly or even hearing from Him at all. Eve was forced to think back over God's instructions to remember what He *really* said to them about the fruit of the trees.

Then, the devil created doubt in Eve's mind by telling her she wouldn't actually die but that she would become like God.

In her mind the only form of death she considered was physical, but the devil knew she would die spiritually and be separated from God. The devil knew exactly what he was doing because he had experienced the very same thing—he sought to exalt himself above God and was punished by eternal separation from Him.

Not having the knowledge of good and evil allowed Adam and Eve to remain in perfect peace and have such closeness with God, but the devil likes to take what is good and distort it. Yes, God did want to keep them from that knowledge, but the devil has a way of making the truth seem cruel. God wanted to protect them from evil and keep them in perfect relation to Himself, but the devil wanted them to think that God was keeping something good from them and causing them to miss out on a life that could be better.

The devil is still using that same tactic to attack our minds today. We live in a fallen world, and the devil is the god of this world. He knows this world promotes sin, immoral lifestyles, and unrealistic standards, and he uses them all to steal our peace. The devil wants to confuse us by distorting the truth and making it seem cruel. Instead of speaking truth concerning sin and immoral lifestyles, the devil wants us to believe the lie that tolerance and acceptance are how we should show love to others. Instead of measuring our lives against God's unchanging standards, the devil wants us to strive to meet the world's ever-changing, ever-compromising standards, which will always leave us feeling discouraged and defeated.

While our enemy is relentless in his pursuit to steal our peace, our weapon is far greater! Because you have the Holy Spirit living inside of you, peace can be permanent. Galatians 5 explains that the fruit of the spirit is peace. Ephesians 4:3 instructs us to "make every effort to keep yourselves united in the Spirit, binding yourselves together with peace" (NLT). When we are united with the Spirit, we become more like Christ. It is the work of the Holy Spirit that allows us to mature in the Lord, and Ephesians 4:14–15 (NLT) explains what happens when we mature:

> Then we will no longer be immature like children. We won't be tossed and blown about by every wind of new teaching. We will not be influenced when people try to trick us with lies so clever they sound like the truth. Instead, we will speak the truth in love, growing in every way more and more like Christ, who is the head of his body, the church.

The Holy Spirit works within us to strengthen our foundation. It is through a relationship with Him that we have peace and clarity in the midst of confusion in this world. In Acts 13, Paul and Barnabas were traveling across the island of Cyprus preaching the Word of God. When they reached Paphos, the governor invited Paul and Barnabas to visit him because he wanted to hear the Word of God, but there was a sorcerer who tried to interfere to keep the governor from believing the truth. Acts 13:9–10 describes the encounter by saying, "'Saul, also known as Paul, was filled with the Holy Spirit, and he looked the sorcerer in the eye.' Then he said, 'You son of the devil, full of every sort of deceit and fraud, and enemy of all that is good! Will you never stop

The devil wants us to strive to meet the world's ever-changing, ever-compromising standards, which will always leave us feeling discouraged and defeated.

perverting the true ways of the Lord?'" Paul spoke the truth and called out evil, but he was only able to do so because he was first filled with the Holy Spirit. Just as the Holy Spirit had sent them on their journey, He led Paul in that situation to confront an attack from the enemy.

There will be times in our lives when we must be like Paul and follow the prompting of the Holy Spirit to address what is displeasing and sinful in the eyes of the Lord. The devil wants us to believe that every new lifestyle should be accepted and people's individual choices should be supported and valued even if they do not align with biblical truth. However, Ephesians 4:15 is clear that we must speak the truth in love. The only lifestyle and choice we should support and value are those of Christ. Peace never comes by our choices being approved and encouraged among others but only through Jesus being accepted and exalted above all else!

Death by Sacrifice

The devil will do all he can to steal from you, but if he can't get all he wants by stealing, he will resort to killing. Most people immediately think of bloodshed and loss of life when they hear the word *kill*, but the word used in John 10:10 doesn't mean murder. The word for "kill" in this verse is the Greek word *thyō*, which means sacrifice.[1] You see, what the devil can't steal from you he wants you to hand over to him in sacrifice.

But wait, why would anyone be willing to hand anything over to the devil? Revelation 12:9 (NLT) describes him as "the one deceiving the whole world"; therefore, you may not even realize when you're handing something over to him. The Bible describes the transaction in Ephesians 4:27 when it says, "Neither give place to the devil" (KJV). The word "place" in this verse refers to a location or a portion of space marked off.

Giving place to the devil means to give him ground as one army may gain ground from another in a battle. And once the devil has gained ground in a certain area of your life, it becomes a stronghold.

Now that the specific wording has been explained, let's look at how and why someone would give ground to the devil. If you look at the verses that surround Ephesians 4:27, you will see several things a person can do to give up ground. Scripture instructs people to stop telling lies, not be controlled by anger, not use foul language, not be deceitful, not be lustful, and so on. All these things give place to the devil because he seeks to kill your purpose and your testimony.

One of the devil's greatest tactics for killing a person's purpose and testimony is stress and exhaustion. Daniel 7:25 says that our enemy "shall wear out the saints of the most High" (KJV), which means he wants you to be so tired that you don't even realize what you're giving up. If he can get you completely distracted and overwhelmed by the world, he knows that your focus will shift from divine purpose to daily plans. The devil is fine with you declaring God with your mouth because he's more interested in you damaging your testimony with your actions and behaviors.

The unrealistic expectations and the unhealthy pace of this world can cause people to compromise in one way or another. Many people are guilty of overscheduling and overcommitting their time which leaves them with little margin for needed rest and quiet time with the Lord. The devil wants the pressure of daily life to build in such a way that people begin to compromise by telling little white lies here and there, responding in anger to situations, saying foul or hurtful things in the moment, and even entertaining lustful thoughts as a way of coping with stress.

The devil is smart enough to know that most people aren't

willing to dive right into sin when they are trying to live the Christian life, but he knows that overwhelming God's people with the stress of this world and turning their focus inward to their own circumstances will cause them to compromise in difficult situations and leave them giving up ground little by little. Lying becomes a stronghold because one lie usually requires another to be told. The angry outbursts continue to be a common response. Coping mechanisms that began as innocent scrolling turn into inappropriate interactions. Without even realizing it, a person can give away more than they ever intended.

Jim Cymbala once said, "Satan is not out to get you to *follow* him; he's out to get you to *ignore* him. When we spiritually zone out, doze off, fall asleep, we are forgetting that we are in the middle of a war—and Satan loves it this way!"[2] Your enemy wants you to become so focused on all the things happening in this physical world that you forget about the war being waged in the spiritual world. Satan wants to operate unnoticed in the shadows of your daily life, in those areas that are frustrating and draining.

When you become exhausted, stressed, and overwhelmed by the demands of life and the busyness of your schedule, you must rely on the strength of the Holy Spirit and seek to maintain closeness with God. If you turn to the world for relief, you will come to realize that little white lies, one little drink, innocent flirting, and a few choice words can cost you more than you ever wanted to pay. Because once you have sinned, the devil will begin accusing you of not being worthy of salvation and convincing you that you've messed up too much to be used by God.

Revelation 12:10 (NLT) describes the devil as "the one who accuses them before our God day and night." He wants you to believe that you are no good after you have sinned. Once you believe his lies and accusations, you no longer strive to live the Christian life because you feel as though you've failed. The devil loves to whisper discouragement, such as, "What makes you think you can teach Bible study now that you've messed up?" "Why would anyone believe what God has done in your life when you fell in sin?" and "How could you set foot back in that church when everyone knows what you've done?"

Continuing to believe his lies instead of turning back to God when you've fallen to sin only results in you sacrificing your purpose and your testimony to the devil. But that is not God's plan for your life! He knew in advance that you would mess up and chose to send His Son to die for you anyways. God doesn't expect you to be perfect, but He longs for you to turn from sin and return to Him. You don't have to believe the lies of the enemy no matter how far from God you have wandered.

When faced with difficult situations and the stress of this world, remember that you have the Holy Spirit as your greatest weapon and strongest defense. Relying on Him above all else will help you recognize Satan's lies, and His presence will cause your heart to be sensitive to His promptings to flee from temptation. Don't let the devil kill your purpose. Whether you are currently struggling to withstand the devil or you have already fallen to sin because of his deceitful tactics, you can lean on the Holy Spirit to defend you in battle and lead you to victory, because He has a great plan and purpose for your life!

Destroy by Division

I wish I could say that stealing and killing is all the devil wants to do in a person's life, but the Bible is clear that he wants to steal, kill, *and* destroy. The enemy wants to accomplish all three things in the life of every person; therefore, he won't stop at anything short of destruction. He wants to steal your peace by attacking your mind, he wants to kill your purpose to leave you feeling worthless and defeated, but he also wants to destroy every good thing in your life and the lives of those closest to you.

The devil would love nothing more than to end your life before you are able to accomplish anything for God, but he can't kill you before it is your time to die. Job 14:5 says, "You have decided the length of our lives. You know how many months we will live, and we are not given a minute longer"; therefore, Satan doesn't have the power to end your life when he wants, but he can try his hardest to destroy it by attacking your health and your home.

Years ago there was a lady in our church named Ida who came to me and said that she had committed to praying for me daily. She explained, "The Lord came to me and said, 'Pray for Pastor Benny because the devil is going to try to kill him.'" I know the Holy Spirit led her to pray, because it was a very difficult time in my life when the stress of ministry was so high and I was not taking care of my health like I should have been. I believe the enemy wanted me dead because he knew that if he could strike the shepherd, he could scatter the sheep. I'm so thankful that Ms. Ida was obedient to pray over me as I faced the attacks of the enemy. Though that season of life was very difficult, the Holy Spirit protected me and provided for me every step of the way. The Lord took what the devil meant for bad and used it to teach me a lesson in taking better care of myself by implementing needed rest and healthier habits through diet and exercise. The devil wanted me dead, but as I relied on the power of the Holy Spirit to fight my battle, I came out stronger and in better shape to serve the Lord.

A. W. Tozer once said, "A Spirit-filled church is the target of the enemy. He knows the potential of a Spirit-filled church and that the focus of such a church is the exaltation of Jesus Christ, which the devil hates with a passion."[3] While I wholeheartedly agree with Tozer, I would say that the family is the ultimate target of the enemy, because the church won't be right if the home isn't right. There is nothing the devil hates more than a Spirit-filled home where marriages are built on Jesus Christ and children are being raised to know God and make Him known.

Make no mistake, the devil will lie in the weeds for years to work his process. First, he wants to steal your peace and create confusion or doubt. Then, he wants to use your stressful circumstances to get you to compromise and surrender your purpose. Finally, he wants all of the confusion, doubt, tension, and stress to cause cracks in the foundation of your health and your home.

The enemy loves to create fear through health scares, frustration through financial struggle, distrust through infidelity, and destruction through divorce. He wants to tear apart your family and leave deep wounds in the hearts of husbands, wives, children, family members, and even friends. He wants to destroy your home in an effort to destroy the house of worship. When families are torn apart, the church takes a huge hit because people often become divided and distant. Keep in mind, when the devil attacks you, he has more than you in mind. He knows that hitting you will hurt others.

> *The enemy wants to tear apart your family and leave deep wounds in the hearts of husbands, wives, children, family members, and even friends. But I have great news: you pack a bigger punch than your enemy!*

But I have great news: you pack a bigger punch than your enemy! While knowing the devil's strategies may be intimidating and uncomfortable to consider, you should never be fearful. First John 4:4 says, "The Spirit who lives in you is greater than the spirit who lives in the world" (NLT). When you surrender every battle to the power of the Holy Spirit, you will have victory. Isaiah 59:19 says, "When the enemy shall come in like a flood, the Spirit of the LORD shall lift up a standard against him" (KJV). Regardless of how hard the enemy comes at you, the Holy Spirit is your greatest weapon against every attack Satan attempts on your life!

STEP 2: BATTLE PLAN

Now, let me hasten to say that a weapon of any kind is of no use if you don't know how to use it. Having a gun and seeing a bear won't matter one bit when I'm hunting if I'm not willing and able to shoot. The Holy Spirit is your greatest weapon in defeating the devil, but your battle plan must include familiarizing yourself with the weapon and having the right ammunition.

In Matthew 4, Jesus provides the perfect example of using the right ammunition when fighting against Satan's attacks. After fasting in the desert for forty days and forty nights, the devil came to tempt Jesus, but He had the power of the Holy Spirit on His side. Matthew 4:1 (KJV) says, "Then was Jesus led up of the Spirit into the wilderness to be tempted of the devil." The Holy Spirit knew the temptation would come when Jesus was weary from fasting, and He was with Him through it all. Jesus had the greatest weapon when the enemy came, and He used the right ammunition to defeat every attack. Through the power of the Holy Spirit, Jesus used precise scripture and a persistent spirit to endure temptation and have victory.

Precise Scripture

In traditional Jewish education, boys would have memorized the first five books of the Bible (the Torah) by age ten. Because He was raised in traditional Jewish culture and learned in the synagogues as a child, Jesus knew scripture by memory, and He was able to apply biblical truth to specific situations.

When Satan tried to tempt Jesus in His moment of extreme hunger, Jesus quoted Deuteronomy 8:3: "People do not live by bread alone, but by every word that comes from the mouth of God." Then, Satan tried to tempt Jesus concerning His safety and trust in God, but Jesus responded with Deuteronomy 6:16: "You must not test the LORD your God." Finally, Satan tried to tempt Jesus concerning worship, but Jesus quoted Deuteronomy 6:13: "You must worship the LORD your God and serve only him." For every specific temptation that Jesus faced, He had precise scripture to quote in response.

The same is true for any temptation you might face in life. The Bible is full of scriptures that can help you in times of temptation and suffering. Just as the Holy Spirit was with Jesus to help Him overcome temptation, you have the power and presence of the Holy Spirit within you to prompt your responses and bring to your remembrance precise scriptures to use as powerful ammunition against the devil.

However, you must do exactly what Jesus did—memorize scripture. Reading your Bible for twenty minutes and praying are great habits to incorporate into your daily walk with the Lord, but to be properly prepared for battle, you must commit to studying God's Word and memorizing scripture. Every week or so I write five or six new scriptures that I want to memorize on a sheet of paper and carry it with me everywhere I go. When I get a free moment in traffic, on the treadmill, or in a drive-through, I pull out the paper and recite the scriptures. Once I have them memorized, I create a new sheet of scriptures and start over again. I've learned that the scripture I utilize is the scripture I memorize.

You don't have to memorize entire books of the Bible like traditional Jewish students, but you can memorize scriptures that relate to what you're struggling with or praying about in your season of life. There's an answer for everything in God's Word: lust (Jas. 1:15), worry (Phil. 4:6–7), fear (2 Tim. 1:7), greed (Eccles. 5:10), people pleasing (Prov. 29:25), and insecurity (Eph. 2:10). It's not about how much of the Bible you get through but how much of the Bible gets through you.

Persistent Spirit

When the enemy came to tempt Jesus in Matthew 4, he didn't stop after one attempt. Satan tried three different types of temptation, and each time, Jesus was persistent in responding with scripture. Instead of resorting to His emotions and frustrations, Jesus continued to use the most powerful ammunition He had—God's Word. Hebrews 4:12 says, "For the word of God is alive and powerful. It is sharper than the sharpest two-edged sword" (NLT).

In moments of difficulty and temptation, your words will never be powerful enough to defeat the devil. Only through the power of the Holy Spirit bringing precise scripture to your mind time and time again will you be able to endure attacks from the enemy. Satan is relentless, and he will come back a hundred times if he thinks you will become inconsistent with your battle plan. James 1:12 promises, "God blesses those who patiently endure testing and temptation. Afterward they will receive the crown of life that God has promised to those who love him" (NLT). When you commit to utilizing precise scripture and having a persistent spirit in the midst of spiritual battles, you will experience victory and live with divine peace. The Holy Spirit is your greatest weapon and strongest defense against the enemy's attacks. He will guide you in every circumstance, give you strength to endure, and enlighten your mind to the enemy's schemes. Seek closeness with the Holy Spirit, and rely on His unlimited power to overcome whatever you face in life!

TIME TO REFLECT

- Most of the time, we are well aware of our weaknesses. They will most likely be those areas that the enemy will attack most often. What areas of your life do you consider weak and more susceptible to enemy attacks?

- Has there been a time in your life when you've been so overwhelmed with stress or exhaustion that you've found yourself giving ground to the enemy? If so, what did you hand over, and when did you realize what you were sacrificing? If not, what practical things in your life can you do to prevent yourself from giving ground?

- Which areas of your life do you need to memorize precise scripture for at the moment? What are some creative ways you can implement scripture memorization into your weekly schedule?

CHAPTER 8
LIVING FREE

THROUGHOUT MY MINISTRY I have had the privilege of taking many groups to Israel. I love traveling with others across the Holy Land and bringing the Bible to life by sharing stories from precise locations where Jesus walked with His disciples, preached powerful messages, and performed mighty miracles. Every group always goes to the Garden Tomb, and after I share the history and the Bible story, I slip away from the group to go to the empty tomb. As I stand in that empty tomb, I can't help but think how Romans 8:11 says, "But if the Spirit of him that raised up Jesus from the dead dwell in you, he that raised up Christ from the dead shall also quicken your mortal bodies by his Spirit that dwelleth in you" (KJV). I'm reminded that if the power of the Holy Spirit can raise Jesus from the dead, His power can help me overcome anything I face in this life.

Christians experience victory over death, hell, and the grave through Jesus Christ because His death on the cross and resurrection from the grave canceled our sin debt. Eternity with God is the greatest gift we could ever receive, but God had even more in mind for us. By Jesus ascending to the right hand of the Father, the Holy Spirit came to live inside every believer to help us in our times of need. The Holy Spirit is our strongest defense against the enemy's attacks, and it's His power that gives us victory in battles. While I believe most Christians experience salvation and truly believe their sins are forgiven, many of them struggle to let themselves live in freedom.

SLAVES TO FEAR

The indwelling power of the Holy Spirit allows us to live free from fear and limitations. Max Lucado once said, "The presence of fear does not mean you have no faith. Fear visits everyone. But make your fear a visitor and not a resident."[1] Just because a Christian battles fear does not mean they doubt their salvation or faith in God. While fear may be commonly felt by all Christians at some point, fear cannot become a voice that speaks louder than the Holy Spirit and receives more attention from your mind.

Fear is a very real emotion that consumes many people's lives daily. While conducting some research on fear, I found it interesting that there are somewhere around seven hundred phobias and fears. Many of them are commonly known, such as the fear of spiders, heights, and public speaking. But I was surprised to learn about phobias like the fear of facial hair, chopsticks, and knees—yes, I mean the joints in your legs. People all around the world suffer from all types of phobias and are often crippled by the effects of fear.

With all that is going on in our world today, you don't have to look very far to find something that can quickly drive you to fear. News outlets continually produce stories of war, disease, famine, and crime. Many social media accounts post and share all types of content depicting horrible things happening throughout society. Turn on the TV or pick up your phone to scroll, and in a matter of minutes fear can begin rising in your spirit.

I am reminded of a story about a man who had an extremely large sign in his yard that said Beware of Dog! One day a neighbor was walking by his house and saw a little Teacup Yorkie running across the yard while the man was checking his mail. The neighbor stopped at the mailbox to tell the man, "I hope you know that dog right there isn't going to scare anybody." The man said, "I know, but the sign will!"

That's exactly what the enemy wants to accomplish in every Christian's life—false fear. Satan knows that the "dog" isn't anything to be scared of because it doesn't stand a chance against your strongest defense, but he will settle for creating just enough fear and anxiety to keep you paralyzed. You see, the enemy has nothing to worry about when Christians are too scared to accomplish anything for God. When fear causes paralysis to set in to a Christian's heart, that person won't allow themself to be used as the hands and feet of Christ.

HOW FEAR FUNCTIONS

Two major fears that the enemy uses to paralyze people are the fear of failure and the fear of the future. The devil wants our fear of failure to keep us from accomplishing anything for God, and he often relies on our past mistakes and guilt to keep us fearful of ever stepping out in faith again. He also wants us to fear the future by creating doubt in our minds as well as using anxiety to kill our hopes and dreams. The enemy wants us so consumed by fear that we forget that we are called and favored. If we live our lives from a spirit of fear, we will always see limitations instead of unlimited power and promise.

Paralyzing fear and limitations are not new strategies of

the devil. He's been using the same tactics throughout history. In 1 Samuel 17, Saul's army was preparing for battle as they camped across from the Philistines in the Elah valley. However, the Philistine army had a secret weapon in their champion, Goliath. The Bible says that Goliath came down into the valley day after day to taunt Saul's army and seek a one-on-one battle with any Israelite soldier. If any of Saul's men could defeat Goliath, the Philistines would become slaves to the Israelites. The deal may have been tempting to some, but 1 Samuel 17:11 explains, "When Saul and the Israelites heard this, they were terrified and deeply shaken" (NLT).

For forty days Goliath said, "Give me a man," but the Israelite army was paralyzed by fear. Saul's army feared failure because they chose to focus on Goliath's track record instead of God's promises. Though Goliath was over nine feet tall, he didn't have God on his side. When young David arrived on the battlefield, he brought a different perspective. Instead of referring to Goliath as a giant, he said, "Who is this uncircumcised Philistine." David also chose to focus on his own track record rather than worrying about Goliath's. He boldly proclaimed, "The LORD who delivered me from the paw of the lion and from the paw of the bear will deliver me from the hand of this Philistine" (1 Sam. 17:37). His victorious past gave him courage for future battles.

First Samuel 16:13 (NLT) says, "So as David stood there among his brothers, Samuel took the flask of olive oil he had brought and anointed David with the oil. And the Spirit of the LORD came powerfully upon David from that day on." David wasn't paralyzed by fear when faced with difficulty, because he was filled with the power of the Holy Spirit! While Saul's army experienced victory over the Philistines and made slaves out of their soldiers, the Israelite soldiers remained slaves to their fear and missed an opportunity to experience the true freedom that comes from putting your trust in the Holy Spirit.

Another example of being bound by fear can be seen in Numbers 13 when Moses sends twelve scouts to go explore the land of Canaan for forty days to report on the conditions and the people who live there. While the scouts reported about the bountiful land "flowing with milk and honey" (Num. 13:27, NLT), ten of them advised that the land should be avoided because "the people living there are powerful, and their towns are large and fortified. We even saw giants there, the descendants of Anak!" (v. 28, NLT). Those ten scouts chose to be led by fear of the future instead of faith in the Father.

Joshua and Caleb were the only two men to suggest that the Israelites take the land of Canaan because they believed God's promises and relied on His power above their own strength and ability. In Numbers 14:24, the Lord specifically described Caleb by saying, "He had another spirit with him, and hath followed me fully" (KJV). Caleb had the power of the Holy Spirit within him, which allowed him to speak boldly, saying, "He will bring us safely into that land and give it to us....Do not rebel against the LORD, and don't be afraid of the people of the land. They are only helpless prey to us! They have no protection, but the LORD is with us! Don't be afraid of them!" (vv. 8–9, NLT). Both men chose to believe in the future God had promised them instead of allowing their circumstances to breed worry and doubt.

Because the Israelites chose to ignore God's voice and doubt His promises, God said, "Because you complained against me, every one of you who is twenty years old or older and was included in the registration will die. You will not enter and occupy the land I swore to give you.

The only exceptions will be Caleb son of Jephunneh and Joshua son of Nun" (vv. 29–30). Their fear of the future is what kept them from experiencing all the blessings and provisions God had planned for their lives. The same is true today, if we let a fear of the future control our lives, we will miss out on the Jeremiah 29:11 future that God promises: "'For I know the plans I have for you,' says the Lord. 'They are plans for good and not for disaster, to give you a future and a hope.'"

I remember getting asked to speak to the student body of a college for the first time many years ago. I was honored to be asked, but fear crept into my mind and I began to think, "Who am I to be speaking in an academic setting? Who am I to speak to scholars?" I didn't have much confidence in my speaking abilities, and I became fearful because of my past insecurities from my own educational experiences.

As I drove to speak at the college, I said to God, "What can someone like me, a nobody from nowhere, tell people at a university?" I remember it like it was yesterday, God said, "You can't tell them anything, but I can tell them a lot through you." In that situation, and in all situations, I've realized that it's never about my ability but God's. I'm so thankful that God doesn't disqualify us when we're fearful but rewards us for stepping out in faith and oftentimes, doing things afraid. I often quote Ian Thomas when the fear tries to creep in: "I can't, You never said I could, but You can, and always said You would."

CRIPPLING LIMITATIONS

God's plan for each of our lives is one of hope and abundance. He wants us to live with unlimited power and expectation of all that He can do through us to impact His kingdom. Living in fear only places limitations in our path. Whether we place those limitations on ourselves or they are placed on us by others, we miss out on fulfilling the purpose God has for our lives.

Don't let the enemy deceive you into placing paralyzing limitations on yourself. You must always remember Whose you are and never underestimate the power within you. David could have focused on his small size, his unimportant position, or his age, but he went to the giant in confidence because of the Holy Spirit's unlimited power within him. He could have felt inferior and incapable, but he knew that the Holy Spirit is the great equalizer.

In 1 Samuel 17:45, David confidently told Goliath, "You come to me with sword, spear, and javelin, but I come to you in the name of the Lord of Heaven's Armies—the God of the armies of Israel, whom you have defied. Today the Lord will conquer you, and I will kill you and cut off your head." It was the Lord who gave the victory, and David was just obedient to kill the giant. The power of the Holy Spirit within David allowed him to believe his abilities were limitless because God was on his side!

Living in fear only places limitations in our path. Whether we place those limitations on ourselves or they are placed on us by others, we miss out on fulfilling the purpose God has for our lives.

The Holy Spirit has been the great equalizer in my life. When I first felt the calling to preach, I felt so inferior. I had always been so scared to speak in front of people and had no confidence in myself as a communicator. In every pastoral role I've ever had, the enemy has tried to make me feel inferior and unqualified. I knew that I didn't have some great educational background or prestigious degrees like other pastors. I didn't have a church background or any family history consisting of preachers. I only knew that God's calling was on my life, and I relied on His presence and power to equip me, lead me, and sustain me in all that ministry would require. If it had required money, status, or degrees, I would've been exempt, but there are no requirements for receiving the Holy Spirit. When I accepted Christ, the Holy Spirit came, and I gained unlimited access to everything I would ever need in life!

Just as you can't place limitations on yourself because of fear, don't let others place limitations on you either. David should have been scared to do anything on his own because he had all kinds of limitations placed on him by others. His own father didn't believe in him enough to even acknowledge him when presenting his sons to Samuel. His brothers degraded him on the battlefield by calling him nosey and telling him to go back to his *few* sheep. King Saul had no confidence in him and said that he was just a boy who was no match for a giant. The giant ridiculed him and laughed in disbelief at his confidence.

I can imagine the devil whispering in David's ear, "Don't even think about it. You'll never defeat that giant. Look around you, no one believes in you. You are way too little, you're *just* a shepherd, you have no military experience, and there isn't a single person who thinks you can accomplish anything great." The lack of confidence from others and their limitations on him could have caused David to fear failure and doubt God's promises about his future. But instead of living discouraged, he chose to value God's opinion of him over anyone else's.

When I was a little boy, I can remember my stepfather always introducing people to our family by saying, "These are *my* children, and Benny is my stepson." He not only made it very clear that I wasn't his child, but he made sure I knew exactly what he thought about me too. He constantly told me that I was stupid and couldn't learn, I could never do anything right, and that I would never amount to anything in life. His opinions of me had a great impact on my early development. I struggled in school because I had grown to believe that I was stupid and couldn't learn.

It wasn't until I got saved and the power of the Holy Spirit came into my heart and life that I began to replace everyone else's opinions with the truth of God's Word. Only through the Holy Spirit working within me have I been able to get victory over deep insecurities in my life. He has allowed me to live free from the fear and limitations that the enemy tries to use on God's children to keep us from experiencing God's perfect plan for our lives.

BREAKING THE CHAINS

The devil wants nothing more than for God's people to live in affliction when we are under attack from the enemy and live in anxiety when we're not. However, the Bible is clear about God's desire for how we should live, because 2 Timothy 1:7 says, "For God hath not given us the spirit of fear; but of power, and of love, and of a sound mind" (KJV). We have power over our enemy because the Holy Spirit lives inside of us!

Before leaving this world, Jesus told His disciples not to be fearful. He knew all the trials they would soon face, and He gave them encouraging words in John 14:27: "I am leaving you with a gift—peace of mind and heart. And the peace I give is a gift the world cannot give. So don't be troubled or afraid." The Holy Spirit is that gift of peace of mind and heart!

Jesus' words of comfort are for us as well. He knows that we will be faced with difficult circumstances that will cause us fear. Yes, fear may be concerning, but it can't become controlling. If you allow fear to control your life, you will find yourself doing things that you shouldn't do. To truly live free from the control of fear and limitations, you must closely follow Jesus and carefully filter your thoughts.

CLOSELY FOLLOW

Just as David had a giant to face, I'm aware that you have giants of your own that you must face. Though David experienced victory over Goliath, he went on to face many other difficult circumstances throughout his life. The enemy doesn't give up simply because he has been defeated in the past. In the same way, you can't grow slack in preparing for a spiritual battle just because you've been victorious in the past.

Luke 4:13 says, "When the devil had finished tempting Jesus, he left him until the next opportunity came." The devil didn't leave for good, because his nature is to lie in wait for another perfect opportunity to lead you astray. Your destruction is way too valuable for the devil to ever accept defeat; he will try and try again. Don't let victory go to your head, but remain vigilant and closely follow Jesus in all that you do.

To truly live free from the control of fear and limitations, you must closely follow Jesus and carefully filter your thoughts.

While you can always rely on God's track record, you can't rely on your own. Just because you have closely followed Jesus for a long time doesn't mean you aren't capable of drifting. Hosea 11:7 says, "My people are bent on turning away from me." Without completely surrendering to the Holy Spirit daily and relying on a fresh filling of His power, you are vulnerable to the enemy's attacks because you are no match for his deceitful tactics. Even those closest to Jesus struggled to closely follow Him at all times.

As Jesus and the disciples eat the Passover meal in Luke 22, Jesus predicts Peter's denial. Of course, Peter insists that he would never do such a terrible thing, he's fully committed to the Lord. But just a few verses later, Luke 22:54 explains the arrest of Jesus by stating, "So they arrested him and led him to the high priest's home," but the verse includes that "Peter followed at a distance." Before the difficulty and danger became apparent, Peter was ready to go to jail with Jesus. However, when the time came to prove his loyalty by closely following Him, Peter allowed the circumstances to create distance between himself and Jesus. Peter became fearful instead of faithful.

Our closeness to the Lord is just like any other earthly relationship, we have a responsibility when it comes to maintaining closeness. I'm reminded of an older married couple named Chester and Martha. They were riding in Chester's old truck one day and came to a red light. Martha looked out her window and saw a young couple in the next car over. The young girl was sitting right up beside the young man driving the vehicle. Martha looked over at Chester and said, "I remember how it used to be that way with me and you." Chester looked over to Martha and said, "I haven't moved."

The same is true about God, He hasn't moved. And just to be clear, He never will move away from you. What started out as distance with Peter eventually led to denial. Letting fear control your life will cause you to follow at a distance. We all get in trouble when we're distant from God. As I've said before, you can be as close to God as you want to be, but what begins by desire must be maintained by discipline. Closely following God happens through an intentional relationship with the Holy Spirit.

When you get the unexpected diagnosis or the job is terminated or the relationship ends, don't let fear of the future create distance between you and God. When distance occurs long enough, denial can creep into your mind. You may find yourself saying, "God's not going to heal me," "God isn't concerned about what career I choose," or, "God doesn't have a person out there for me." Instead of allowing your emotions to direct your path, rely on the Holy Spirit to not only bring you comfort but to provide wisdom for how you should navigate every situation.

Remember that what is a surprise to you has never been a surprise to God. He saw your difficulty and began working it out before you ever knew it was a part of His plan for your life. Allowing fear to control your situation never makes things easier to navigate.

I can't express how important it is to not only rely on the Holy Spirit in difficult circumstances but to surround yourself with the right people who are also closely following Jesus. Peter followed at a distance and began to fellowship around the fire with the wrong crowd. He wasn't with the other disciples but was surrounded by people who didn't follow Jesus.

Proverbs 13:20 says, "Walk with the wise and become wise; associate with fools and get in trouble." Surrounding yourself with other like-minded Christians is so important in the midst of trials because they will pull you along when you're weak and encourage you to closely follow the Lord. I've learned that if you hang around a barber shop, you'll get a haircut. If you lie with dogs, you'll get fleas. If you associate with others who follow afar off, you'll find yourself distant as well. If you don't already have those people in your life, seek wisdom from the Holy Spirit in choosing the right friends and mentors. Pray for the right people who will hold you accountable and remind you of truth.

CAREFULLY FILTER

No one has ever followed God as closely as Jesus did on earth, yet the enemy still attacked Him at every opportunity. Closely following God is so important, but you must also carefully filter your thoughts because the devil will take every opportunity to create fear and doubt in your mind. Even when you're following closely, you can still stumble.

Second Corinthians 10:5 tells us to "take every thought captive to obey Christ." This verse is used when talking about fighting a spiritual battle. When you take every thought captive to Christ, you are using "divine power to destroy strongholds" (v. 4). The enemy wants to gain ground in your mind and create strongholds through fear, but when you allow the Holy Spirit to filter your thoughts and take each one captive, you can have victory over Satan's attacks.

While you can't keep birds from flying over your head, you can keep them from nesting in your hair. In the same way, you can't keep random thoughts from popping into your head, but you don't have to allow them to stay or have an influence in your life. Relying on the Holy Spirit to filter your thoughts will help you decide whether or not a thought should remain or be removed.

When a thought creeps into your mind, the first question you must ask is, "Whose voice is that?" You have to determine if it's your voice, God's voice, or the enemy's voice. Accurately identifying the voice you hear will require you to filter that thought to see if it aligns with God's character and His promises.

You have a clever enemy, so some thoughts may take more filtering than others.

Remember, Satan loves to twist and manipulate the truth to trip you up. In some cases, the Holy Spirit may quickly bring precise scripture to your remembrance that filters your thought for the right voice. However, you may need to dig into God's Word more and seek His divine wisdom.

First, place your thought up against God's character and what you know to be true about Him. Regularly studying the Bible and talking to God in prayer will teach you about His character, and you will fall in love with Who He is. You will also grow more sensitive to the Holy Spirit's promptings for you to remember God's character. Isaiah 40:8 says, "The grass withers and the flowers fade, but the word of our God stands forever." And if His Word is true and stands forever, then Malachi 3:6 will always be true of God's character, "I am the Lord, and I do not change."

In the same way, James 1:17 assures us of God's character, "Whatever is good and perfect is a gift coming down to us from God our Father, who created all the lights in the heavens. He never changes or casts a shifting shadow." If it's not good and perfect, it's not God. Charles Spurgeon once said, "God is too good to be unkind and He is too wise to be mistaken. And when we cannot trace His hand, we must trust His heart." Even when the most confusing or even fearful thoughts come to your mind, you must ask yourself if the thought aligns with God's Word and His character. If it doesn't align, then it must be your own voice or that of the enemy.

Many times your own voice is going to be selfishly and/ or emotionally driven. Only when placed next to what's true about God will you realize the correct voice. Not all thoughts are bad, but a good thought does not equal a God thought. It takes humility and divine wisdom from the Holy Spirit to point out when thoughts are self-serving instead of God-honoring.

You must determine whether your thoughts align with God's promises as well. Hebrews 10:23 reminds us, "Let us hold tightly without wavering to the hope we affirm, for God can be trusted to keep his promise." Therefore, you can always rely on God's promises in the Bible when filtering your thoughts.

In Matthew 6, God promises to sufficiently provide your daily portion. He gives you "daily bread," and He warns you against worrying about the future. If thoughts enter your mind about fearing the future due to a lack of provision, you know that isn't God's voice. God promises to provide everything you need.

Thoughts may come to your mind about loneliness. The enemy wants you to believe that you are all alone in your circumstances, but Isaiah 41:10 says, "Don't be afraid, for I am with you. Don't be discouraged, for I am your God. I will strengthen you and help you. I will hold you up with my victorious right hand." Maybe you are walking through a divorce or the loss of a close friend. The enemy wants you to dwell on your emotions and hear the voice of negativity telling you that you're all alone and no one cares, but you can look to God's promises to filter that thought. You can be encouraged that God is with you, gives you strength, and holds you when you're at your weakest and loneliest.

God does not want you to live a life bound to fear and limitations. He wants you to remember the spirit He has given you and rely on the Holy Spirit's power to lead you in the path of freedom. You are a child of the Most High, not a slave who is tormented by enemy attacks. You are chosen, forgiven, loved, favored, and equipped

God does not want you to live a life bound to fear and limitations. He wants you to remember the spirit He has given you and rely on the Holy Spirit's power to lead you in the path of freedom.

by God. He has great plans for your life, which is why you must be prepared for battle and able to defend against the enemy's attacks. The power within you is so much greater than that of the enemy, but you must access that power through closeness with the Holy Spirit. It is only through a close, intentional relationship with Him that you can overcome fear and limitations to truly live free!

TIME TO REFLECT

- Have there been situations in your life when you have felt paralyzed by fear? What caused you to become paralyzed, and how did you begin to move forward?

- How have the opinions of others impacted your decisions or actions in life? Do you find yourself being influenced more by the limitations you place on yourself or limitations that others place on you?

- What type of situations cause you or may cause you to follow from afar? Are there people in your life who influence you to follow from a distance more than you intend?

CHAPTER 9
INDESCRIBABLE BOLDNESS

T HE MORNING AFTER I accepted Jesus into my heart, I experienced emotions that I had never felt in any situation in my life. I shared this story in my book *Defy the Odds*, but I believe it bears repeating in the context of the Holy Spirit being at work in my heart and life.

I didn't realize it at the time, but the transforming power of the Holy Spirit began a divine work in my heart and life immediately after salvation. I remember lying in my bed early the next morning, planning to keep my salvation a secret from my friends. I had decided to be my old self around my friends but be my new self when I was at home, at church, or alone. Little did I know, the Holy Spirit wasn't going to let me get away with such a plan.

When I pulled up to the gas station the next morning and saw all my buddies standing around, something inside me caused me to walk right up to them and say, "Boys, the greatest thing happened to me last night. I got saved! I gave my life to Jesus!" At the time, I had no idea where my outburst had come from, but I know now that the Holy Spirit led me to tell them that I was a new person. By His power alone was I able to begin my walk with the Lord on the right foot. It wasn't me, but the Holy Spirit within me, that gave me indescribable boldness to speak about my salvation. And He's continued to fill me with boldness to witness and reach people for Jesus ever since that day!

The Holy Spirit came into my life and replaced my shy, discouraged nature with courage and determination that had never before been a part of my personality. Instead of hiding from people and avoiding situations where I would have to speak in front of others, I found myself at the Rescue Mission and nursing homes, taking every opportunity to share the gospel with anyone who would listen. I even agreed to preach a Sunday night service at our church to see if I truly felt a calling to preach.

Now, I'm certainly not saying that I got saved and never made mistakes. I have stumbled along the way, but God has been so good to dust me off and get me back to work. The boldness I've had has never been tied to my own abilities or desires but has always been the result of the power of the Holy Spirit living within me and using me to fulfill my purpose in life.

BEYOND FAILURE

Some people think that a person becomes a Christian, receives the power of the Holy Spirit, and is used by God to accomplish great things as long as they don't make any big mistakes. When failure happens in a person's life, it doesn't disqualify them from receiving

I'm so thankful that we serve a God who's in the business of picking people up and declaring them chosen and called, even in light of their failures.

God's grace, mercy, favor, calling, or power on their life. Yes, people have to live with the unpleasant consequences of their mistakes, but God never said that failure takes you out of the game for good.

The Holy Spirit gives us the boldness to live for Christ and share the gospel even after failure. Just in case you weren't aware, we all fail and fall short. Some people's failures are public, while others are private to the eyes of the world—but God sees it all the same. The world loves to kick a person when they're down and declare someone "canceled" because they've made mistakes, but I'm so thankful that we serve a God who's in the business of picking people up and declaring them chosen and called, even in light of their failures. Through the power of the Holy Spirit, we can all begin again!

Many Christians never fully experience the boldness that comes from the Holy Spirit because they can't see beyond their past failures. Other Christians walk in boldness to share the gospel, but if failure happens, they're reluctant to ever step out again. Regardless of how and when failure has happened in a person's life, if they're not dead, God's not done! God loves to use the most unlikely people who the world has cast aside to do the most incredible things for His kingdom.

THE FAITHFUL FAILED

Moses and Paul (formerly Saul) are two incredible examples of how God calls the unlikely and uses people who had pretty big mistakes in their past. Moses was a murderer but God still called Him to lead the people of Israel out of bondage and into the promised land. In describing Moses committing murder, Exodus 2:12 says, "After looking in all directions to make sure no one was watching, Moses killed the Egyptian and hid the body in the sand." This verse proves that Moses didn't accidentally kill the man due to a physical altercation that got out of hand. Moses intentionally killed the Egyptian. Yet when God needed someone to lead the rescue of His people, Moses was His first choice. It wasn't Moses' past reputation, present ability, or even willingness that qualified him for the job, it was God's presence with him that made him the worthy choice. Because Moses was led by the powerful presence of the Holy Spirit, he was able to boldly approach Pharoah and demand the release of God's people!

The apostle Paul was once a man who dedicated his life's work to kill Christians. Acts 9:1 says, "Saul was uttering threats with every breath and was eager to kill the Lord's followers." Christians were deeply fearful of encountering Saul because of his reputation as a violent persecutor. In Acts 9, God told Ananias to go find Saul and pray over him, but Ananias replied, "I've heard many people talk about the terrible things this man has done to the believers in Jerusalem! And he is authorized by the leading priests to arrest everyone who calls upon your name." Understandably, Ananias was afraid of what could happen if he got anywhere near Saul.

However, God saw beyond Saul's past to see Paul's purpose, the man who arguably did more to shape Christianity than anyone other than Jesus Christ.

When Ananias obeyed the Lord and prayed over Saul, he said, "Brother Saul, the Lord Jesus, who appeared to you on the road, has sent me so that you might regain your sight and be filled with the Holy Spirit" (Acts 9:17). Saul was chosen by God, and after his salvation and baptism, Acts 9:20 explains, "And immediately he began preaching about Jesus in the synagogues, saying, 'He is indeed the Son of God!'" Although Saul's past was full of terrible mistakes, the power of the Holy Spirit within him allowed him to go "all around Jerusalem with them, preaching boldly in the name of the Lord" (Acts

9:28). Boldness is not exclusively given to those with a fairly clean past but given to anyone who will surrender their lives to the power and presence of the Holy Spirit's guidance.

David and Peter have slightly different stories than Moses and Paul. Both were chosen by God to fulfill great kingdom purposes with their lives. However, after following closely with the Lord for many years, the two men found themselves face-to-face with failure. But I'm so glad God really loves a comeback story!

David was God's chosen King, a man after God's own heart, yet he committed adultery and had a man killed. As a young boy, neither David's appearance nor his abilities led anyone to believe that he would become a great leader and a great warrior, well, no one except God. In 1 Samuel, the Lord chose the most unlikely son of Jesse to be the next King of Israel. Verse 13 says, "So as David stood there among his brothers, Samuel took the flask of olive oil he had brought and anointed David with the oil. And the Spirit of the Lord came powerfully upon David from that day on." He was God's chosen king many years before he would ever sit on the throne.

The Lord referred to David as "a man after his own heart" (1 Sam. 13:14). But just as we all do at some point in our lives, he fell to temptation. Now, I'm not saying everyone fails in the same way David did, but we all mess up. Sin is sin to God, we're the ones who place sin on a scale. God sees all sin the same because all sin separates us from God regardless of how bad we deem the sin. If people are not careful, they'll create a sin scale where their own sin always falls just below the "too bad" line, and they'll miss out on restoration that comes only through repentance.

It kind of reminds me of the man who went to the doctor and said, "Doc, I've been having these terrible headaches, and I just can't figure out what the problem is. I don't smoke like other people. I don't drink like others do. I don't stay out late partying or carousing like some do. I don't overeat like a lot of people do. Doc, I just can't figure out the problem." The doctor responded, "Oh, I know exactly what the problem is— your halo is on too tight."

We all fall short, but we can learn a lesson from David's response to failure. Although he sinned greatly, he experienced restoration because he repented his sin and asked God to restore him. Psalm 51 is David's psalm of repentance after he committed adultery with Bathsheba. In Psalm 51:1, David says, "Have mercy on me, O God, because of your unfailing love. Because of your great compassion, blot out the stain of my sins." Notice that David doesn't assume that he has done anything to deserve forgiveness. He begins by clearly stating that it is only because of God's love and compassion that David can be forgiven.

In verses 10–12, David asks God, "Create in me a clean heart, O God. Renew a loyal spirit within me. Do not banish me from your presence, and don't take your Holy Spirit from me. Restore to me the joy of your salvation, and make me willing to obey you." David had first-hand knowledge of the Holy Spirit's ability to leave a person. First Samuel 16:14 says, "Now the Spirit of the Lord had left Saul," because he had disobeyed God. David didn't want the same fate, so he pleaded with God to not only forgive his sins but restore his soul.

While David certainly needed God to forgive him of his sins, he also knew that the presence of the Holy Spirit can only dwell within a pure heart. When a person's spirit is right with the Lord, there is closeness, intimacy, and joy that cannot be felt through any earthly relationship. David knew that sin had created distance and depression. The Lord's presence wasn't with him as it had once been, and he was desperate for restoration that would allow him to fellowship once again with the Holy Spirit.

Because of his willingness to confess sin, repent, and seek restoration, God continued to keep His hand of blessing on David's life. Though David endured the earthly consequences of his failures, he trusted God and continued to lead with boldness. He never shrank from his role or responsibilities, but instead, he continued to courageously follow the Lord. The world may have only been able to see a king with a sinful past, but God saw the future of David's wise son, Solomon, and even further to God's own son, our Savior, Jesus!

Another example of restoration can be seen in the life of Peter. In the previous chapter, I talked about how Peter followed Jesus afar off, hung out with the wrong crowd, and denied Jesus three times. By most people's standards, he failed in a big way. I mean who can be that close to Jesus one minute and deny him the next minute? I know who... me and you. We may not say out loud, "I don't know Jesus," but we can refuse to be used by God in certain situations or we can refrain from sharing Jesus with someone when the opportunity arises. While most Christians don't go around denying Jesus with their words, many deny Him more than three times with their thoughts and actions. If we're all honest, we are more like Peter than we want to admit.

While Peter failed greatly, God had the greatest comeback story for his life! And it didn't involve a five-year, twenty-step process to restore him to "useful" status in ministry once again. Humans often like to assign a set of foolproof steps or a lengthy process to different kinds of rehabilitation or restoration. I'm not saying a process doesn't work, but I am saying that if we're not careful, we will disqualify someone or place them on hold based on human standards when that person may already be fully forgiven and restored in God's eyes. We must remember that Acts 10:15 says, "But the voice spoke again: 'Do not call something unclean if God has made it clean.'" We can see only the outer appearance of a person, but only God can see a person's heart and the sincerity in their repentance. In Peter's case, the only thing that disqualified him from continuing in ministry was his proximity to Jesus.

Because he grew distant from the Lord, Peter ended up going back to his old way of life. He saw himself as disqualified from ministry, so he went back to fishing. But even in backsliding, his ability to lead others was undeniable because he was born to influence people.

John 21:3 says, "Simon Peter said, 'I'm going fishing.' 'We'll come, too,' they all said. So they went out in the boat" (NLT). Instead of using his influence to lead others to Jesus, Peter influenced others to return to their old ways. Without the presence of the Lord in his life, Peter had no confidence in his God-given abilities. He believed that his failures ruined his future so he resorted to the life he lived in his past.

If we're not careful, we will disqualify someone or place them on hold based on human standards when that person may already be fully forgiven and restored in God's eyes.

What I love most about Peter's story is how intentional Jesus was in making sure Peter knew he was forgiven and was still called and qualified to build His kingdom! I love that when Mary Magdalene arrived at the empty tomb, the angel instructed her, in Mark 16:7, to "go and tell his disciples, *including Peter*, that Jesus is going ahead of you to Galilee" (emphasis added). Regardless of Peter's denial of Jesus, God never denied Peter nor did He love him any less.

Even though Peter went back to his old life, Jesus went after him again and stood on the shoreline ready to lead him back to his true calling. Jesus is all-knowing, but He was strategic in getting Peter to reaffirm all that he had previously denied. When Jesus appeared to the disciples on the shoreline and made them breakfast, He asked Peter three different times, "Simon son of John, do you love me?" (John 21:16), not because He needed to hear Peter say those words but because Peter needed to hear himself reaffirm his faith and commitment to Jesus. Saying those words out loud helped to restore Peter's weary, weeping heart. With each affirmation, Peter grew more and more confident in his words being true and in his dedication to a life of ministry. Jesus knows just what we need in our lowest times, and He is so faithful to reach down and restore us to the life and path He created for us!

Within six short weeks, Peter went from a cowardly disciple to a bold apostle. What made all the difference? The powerful presence of the Holy Spirit! Jesus couldn't remain in close proximity to every disciple while they fulfilled their calling to "go into all the world and preach the Good News to everyone" (Mark 16:15). Therefore, He sent the Holy Spirit to dwell within every believer and give them the power to reach the world for Jesus!

Acts 2:1–4 describes the moment that the Holy Spirit came to dwell within every believer:

> On the day of Pentecost all the believers were meeting together in one place. Suddenly, there was a sound from heaven like the roaring of a mighty windstorm, and it filled the house where they were sitting. Then, what

looked like flames or tongues of fire appeared and settled on each of them. And everyone present was filled with the Holy Spirit.

It was from that moment on that Peter had an indescribable boldness about him when it came to sharing the gospel. As the crowds witnessed the effects of the Holy Spirit coming, people began to shout in disbelief claiming that the believers were drunk.

However, Acts 2:14–15 shows that Peter was the one to boldly speak up, "Then Peter stepped forward with the eleven other apostles and shouted to the crowd, 'Listen carefully, all of you, fellow Jews and residents of Jerusalem! Make no mistake about this. These people are not drunk, as some of you are assuming.'" Then, in verse 37, scripture makes the effects of Peter's boldness clear: "Peter's words pierced their hearts, and they said to him and to the other apostles, 'Brothers, what should we do?'" The incredible power of the Holy Spirit gave Peter an undeniable boldness when addressing the opposing crowd and proclaiming Jesus Christ as Lord and Savior!

A FUTURE BEYOND FAILURE

You see, when it comes to the Christian life, you will make your fair share of mistakes, but it is only through a relationship with the Holy Spirit that you can experience restoration and redemption. Mistakes do not disqualify you from ministry. The power with which you are able to live the Christian life and serve Jesus is not in yourself but through the Holy Spirit. When He calls you, He equips you. And no one can disqualify you from what the Lord has called you to do—not even you. When failure happens, confess your sins to Jesus, repent, and surrender your life once again to the Holy Spirit. Allow Him complete control to lead your every decision and be obedient to walk in His way. Then, you will have indescribable boldness to live out the God-given calling on your life!

Jesus told twelve uneducated men who had never been more than fifty miles or so away from Galilee to "go into all the world and preach the Good News to everyone" (Mark 16:15). They were not perfect men by any means. Some struggled with doubt, others with faith, and some with pride, but God used them anyway. Why? Because there are no perfect people. The twelve disciples certainly didn't have the wisdom, biblical knowledge, or speaking abilities to successfully take the gospel to the *whole world*. It was only through the power of the Holy Spirit.

Acts 4:13 says, "The members of the council were amazed when they saw the boldness of Peter and John, for they could see that they were ordinary men with no special training in the Scriptures." "Ordinary men" is a nice way of saying that people thought they were ignorant, but God loves to use the most unlikely people. Only by the power of the Holy Spirit did these men have such boldness that left everyone in amazement.

The Holy Spirit is Who makes all the difference. Whether you have failed in the past, are currently following afar off, or will eventually make a mistake in the future, rest assured that God loves you in spite of your failures and has a unique purpose for your life. Failures and mistakes may redirect your path a little and leave you with uncomfortable consequences, but God doesn't disqualify you from serving Him. The Holy Spirit wants to come into your heart once more to renovate and remodel His dwelling place. If you will allow Him, He will remove all that doesn't glorify God and restore you to active duty in sharing the gospel and ministering to others!

When a dear friend of mine was going through a very dark

and difficult time, I made a decision to stick by his side and provide encouragement through sharing scripture and godly advice as well as praying with him and for him. Too often, godly people are cast aside when they make mistakes and those closest to them are suddenly nowhere to be found. He had been in ministry for many years, but because of some mistakes he had made in the past, he had been removed from his position in ministry and began to doubt if God would ever be able to use him again.

Over the course of many months, he had gone through counseling and received advice from godly mentors in his life. More than anything, he sought closeness with the Lord like never before. He allowed the power of the Holy Spirit to work within him to bring him to the point of restoration and redemption. Although he had experienced great spiritual renewal, many in the Christian community would continue labeling him "canceled" due to his mistakes. I knew this weighed heavy on his heart and mind, and the enemy made every attempt to keep him from believing that he would ever get another opportunity to boldly serve God in ministry.

I accompanied my friend on a trip to Kansas to shoot a video that would detail his return to ministry. As we wrapped up the video shoot, I started talking with one of the young guys on the film team. He proceeded to tell me that his wife had been diagnosed with cancer recently. I wanted to encourage his heart to believe God for healing, so I shared with him how God had healed my wife of seizures many years ago. I asked everyone to gather around for prayer over this young man and his wife. As we all prayed together, the presence of God came in a mighty way. After we prayed, I felt like the Holy Spirit told me to ask the worship leader to lead everyone in a song. He began to sing the old hymn, "Great Is Thy Faithfulness." As we sang those precious lyrics—"Morning by morning new mercies I see"—I looked over to see my friend singing with tears rolling down his face.

After we wrapped up the trip and headed back home, I received a text from my friend the next day that said, "You obeyed the Lord in asking the worship leader to sing because Psalm 51:12–13 came to my mind during that song, and the Lord restored the joy of my salvation!" He went on to explain that his circumstances had left him feeling disqualified from sharing the gospel, but the Holy Spirit had worked in that moment to restore a right spirit within him and bring joy back to his soul! The morning after that trip, my friend shared the gospel with someone for the first time since being removed from his ministry position. The Holy Spirit had brought restoration and had given him a renewed boldness to walk in his God-given purpose!

If you have accepted Jesus as Savior, the Holy Spirit has placed unlimited boldness within you. However, you must be willing to walk in that boldness and be obedient to whatever the Holy Spirit leads you to do. You can walk in boldness regardless of failure if you commit to honest confession, accept forgiveness, and return to your post.

LIVING BOLDLY

To truly live out your purpose with boldness, you must prioritize honest confession. When facing failure, you cannot hold anything back when it comes to confessing your sin. You cannot blame anything or anyone else for the choices you have made. Make to attempt to excuse your actions. The only posture to have when coming to the Lord in repentance is one of humility and anguish over your sin. Psalm 51 teaches us that a broken and repentant heart cannot be refused by God. You must follow

David's example of honest confession, and while you may ask God to spare you any spiritual consequences, you must willingly accept the earthly consequences. Your only desire must be a right relationship with God instead of a right standing or pleasant appearance in the eyes of others.

Only broken things can be mended and repaired. You will never live out your purpose with boldness if you only ask for a fresh coat of paint to cover the knicks and dings. Boldness comes through the Holy Spirit putting you back together stronger than you ever were on your own. Just as a bone heals stronger after a break, you will be restored with the strength and power of the Holy Spirit when you come to the Lord with an honest confession. Maybe there are things from your past that you have never accepted responsibility for or confessed with honesty. Those things may weigh you down and keep you from boldly living for Christ. Regardless of when mistakes have happened, there is freedom and restoration that only comes through honest confession.

Truly accepting forgiveness is another key to boldly living the Christian life. Jesus' death on the cross provided forgiveness for every sin, but you must fully accept that forgiveness and live in the freedom that comes from salvation. You can't live boldly while also carrying loads of shame or guilt from past mistakes. Psalm 103:12 says, "He has removed our sins as far from us as the east is from the west," yet many Christians live as if their sins are dragging behind them like weighty chains. Forgiveness in Christ means a clean slate, a fresh start as if the mistakes never happened.

Just as a person can't strut in chains, you can't live boldly while carrying shame. Not that anyone should live with worldly arrogance, but Christians should live with godly confidence. Your head should only be held high in worship, not arrogance, but it should only be bowed in reverence, not disgrace. You are a child of the King and were created to live boldly and confidently because of Whose you are!

When you have honestly confessed your sins and have truly accepted forgiveness, you are ready to activate boldness. It lies within you, but it's up to you whether or not you live from a place of unlimited boldness or crippling apprehension. Just as you can own an umbrella and still get soaked unless you open it, you have access to everything you need to boldly serve the Lord, but you must activate that boldness by stepping outside your comfort zone when the Holy Spirit leads you. In my own experiences, the Holy Spirit hasn't asked me to inch forward very often, but He has asked me to leap out in faith. It is in those moments that we can activate boldness and be obedient to what the Lord has called us to do!

I love to study great preachers, and one of my favorites is Charles Spurgeon, the Prince of Preachers. I once read that as he walked to the pulpit, he would say with every step, "I believe in the Holy Spirit. I believe in the Holy Spirit." It is well known that Spurgeon lived his life, not just when preaching, with a conscious dependence on the power of the Holy Spirit. Spurgeon's example has greatly impacted my life and my preaching. On the pulpit I preach from every Sunday, "I believe in the Holy Spirit" is written across the top so that I see it right above my Bible and my sermon notes. I repeat those words as I walk to the pulpit and I'm reminded of them every time I look down because my greatest desire is for the Holy Spirit to be the only one preaching.

Billy Sunday is another preacher I have studied and looked to when modeling good habits. I learned that Billy Sunday would have his Bible opened to Isaiah 61:1 every time he preached. The verse says, "The Spirit of the Sovereign Lord is upon me, for the

Lord has anointed me to bring good news to the poor. He has sent me to comfort the brokenhearted and to proclaim that captives will be released and prisoners will be freed."

Since reading about this habit of his, I have adapted this practice to fit my sermon preparation every week. After preparing my sermon early in the week, I always lay my sermon notes on a Bible I have in my office that is always opened to Isaiah 61:1 because I never want to forget that the only reason that I am able to prepare a sermon and walk to the pulpit is that the Lord has anointed me and has called me to preach the gospel and pastor people. There is nothing good in me. I have no abilities apart from what the Holy Spirit has gifted me with. I want to live as Spurgeon did with a conscious dependence on the Holy Spirit in everything I do.

If you will surrender your pride, comfort, insecurities, and perceptions to allow the Holy Spirit to fill you with boldness that only comes from closeness with Him, you will be blown away by all that the Lord leads you to do in reaching others for Him!

When I begin every day with the knowledge that I'm equipped, chosen, called, and anointed by God to live out a unique purpose through the unlimited power of the Holy Spirit, I live with an urgency and an indescribable boldness to share Jesus Christ with anyone I meet! The same will be true for your life. If you will surrender your pride, comfort, insecurities, and perceptions to allow the Holy Spirit to fill you with boldness that only comes from closeness with Him, you will be blown away by all that the Lord leads you to do in reaching others for Him!

TIME TO REFLECT

- Has there ever been a time in your life when you have allowed past mistakes to weigh you down and keep you from stepping out in faith? If so, what lies did you believe about your mistakes? What truth from God's Word can you use to replace that lie and begin believing that He will use your life in a mighty way?

- Peter followed afar off and ended up with the wrong crowd. Has there ever been a time in your life when you have followed afar off? How did you feel when distance grew between you and God? What can you do to keep from following afar off again in the future?

- When it comes to living boldly, honest confession of sin can keep you from being afraid to follow the Lord. Is there anything in your own life that you may need to take full responsibility for or confess fully to the Lord? How is honest confession freeing?

PART IV
YOUR UNLIMITED PURPOSE

When the Spirit of truth comes, he will guide you into all truth. He will not speak on his own but will tell you what he has heard. He will tell you about the future.

—John 16:13, NLT

CHAPTER 10
DIVINE DIRECTION

THINK IT IS safe to say that we all have regrets. If you have lived a little, you are certain to have a few regrets, but if you have lived a long time, you probably have more than you would like to admit. Sure, some of us may regret things like not going to a high school dance or not buying those nice shoes when they were on sale. Others may regret spending too much money on a vacation or not studying enough for a big test. I have my own fair share of regrets, but the ones that have caused me to lose the most sleep are the ones that had an eternal impact.

I often talk about pastoring Rock Springs Church and the wonderful growth that has occurred over the thirty-three-plus years I have been the pastor. I never mind sharing about the time I spent pastoring my previous church—Sweeten Hill— where the congregation grew from thirty to more than three hundred in just a few years. But when it comes to sharing about pastoring my very first church, I'm not as comfortable reflecting on my time there.

Let me hasten to say that I never did anything immoral while pastoring the church, but I did the people an injustice by not preaching much on the Holy Spirit or allowing Him to determine the direction of the church. As a young preacher,

I was high energy and low IQ, and I thought I knew everything. What I needed most was the Holy Spirit's power and presence leading my ministry instead of relying on my own strength and limited knowledge as a young pastor. Because of my choices, I know I missed many opportunities to impact the kingdom for eternity in a much greater way.

Jesus said in John 16:13, "When the Spirit of truth comes, he will guide you into all truth. He will not speak on his own but will tell you what he has heard. He will tell you about the future" (NLT). By not preaching more about the Holy Spirit and not allowing Him to guide the direction of the church according to His divine wisdom, I feel responsible for the downfall of my first church. It closed its doors for good, and I believe it is because of choices I made—or even neglected to make—that caused the decline and eventual closure.

I am so grateful that God is a God of second chances. Even though I feel like I failed at pastoring my first church, He used my failure to teach me valuable lessons and prepare me for what He had in store for my future. He has been so faithful in teaching me about the true power of the Holy Spirit in providing a divine direction for our lives that is better than any plan or path we could make for ourselves.

WE HAVE A HELPER

The Holy Spirit is vitally important to your everyday life because the Father is in heaven on the throne and Jesus is at His right hand, but it is the Holy Spirit who is here on Earth as your helper and guide. Without the Holy Spirit, you have no other source for making it through life and accomplishing anything of eternal significance.

The truth of the matter is that you will struggle without

the Holy Spirit. The Christian life isn't difficult but impossible without the Holy Spirit. You simply cannot live life and fulfill your purpose without the Holy Spirit's divine direction guiding you every day.

I'm reminded of a man who was struggling to get his washing machine through the front door of his home right as his next-door neighbor was walking past. The neighbor stopped and asked if he could help. The man breathed a sigh of relief and said, "That would be great! I could really use the help. If you'll get it from the outside, I'll get it from the inside, and we should be able to handle this quickly!"

After five minutes of continual struggle, both men were exhausted. The neighbor wiped the sweat from his forehead and said, "This thing is bigger than it looks. I don't know if we'll ever be able to get it into your house." The man replied, "*Into* my house? I'm trying to get this thing *out* of my house!"

You will struggle without the Holy Spirit

In the same way, we struggle in life when we don't surrender to the Holy Spirit. When we don't live out of our God-given purpose, we will always struggle with frustration and feel unsatisfied in all that we attempt to do. However, we can only live out our purpose through the power and presence of the Holy Spirit in our daily lives. While it sounds easy enough to just surrender to the Holy Spirit's plans since it's what is best for us anyway, there is only one problem—our sinful nature.

Galatians 5:16–17 explains the war between the Spirit and our flesh:

> So I say, let the Holy Spirit guide your lives. Then you won't be doing what your sinful nature craves. The sinful nature wants to do evil, which is just the opposite

> of what the Spirit wants. And the Spirit gives us desires
> that are the opposite of what the sinful nature desires.
> These two forces are constantly fighting each other, so
> you are not free to carry out your good intentions.

Our sinful nature will always crave the opposite of what the Holy Spirit wants for our lives. Therefore, we are in desperate need of a fresh filling and anointing of Holy Spirit power every day to walk in the Spirit instead of our flesh.

Nothing about the world we live in makes it any easier to deny our flesh and live out our divine purpose. Today's culture is in direct opposition of the Holy Spirit because He convicts our hearts and leads us away from our own works and desires and into God's divine plans for our lives. The Holy Spirit constantly tells us that it's not about us, and we don't like that at all. He reminds us again and again that the goal of this life is holiness, not happiness, but all our flesh really wants is pleasure. Our sinful nature says, "We want it our way and we want it now!"

The Holy Spirit calls us to a life of humility and selflessness because our true purpose will always be tied to other people. I wish I could tell you that the battle between the flesh and the Spirit goes away, but in Romans 7:15, Paul writes, "I don't really understand myself, for I want to do what is right, but I don't do it. Instead, I do what I hate." Unless we surrender daily to the Holy Spirit and allow Him to be our helper and our guide, we will fall to our fleshly desires.

HE HELPS US KNOW

The Holy Spirit's role is that of a helper because we are not able to understand anything of eternal significance without the Holy Spirit first giving us the right understanding. 1 John

2:27 says, "But you have received the Holy Spirit, and he lives within you, so you don't need anyone to teach you what is true. For the Spirit teaches you everything you need to know, and what he teaches is true—it is not a lie. So just as he has taught you, remain in fellowship with Christ." We get in trouble when we turn to other things and other people to provide us with a true understanding of our purpose in life. The Holy Spirit helps us know God, the Bible, and our calling in life.

God is a divine, spiritual Being which means our finite, human minds cannot comprehend His thoughts, ways, or words. Without the help of the Holy Spirit, we cannot know God or comprehend the magnitude of Who He is. Ephesians 1:17 explains that we must have "spiritual wisdom and insight so that you might grow in your knowledge of God."

The Holy Spirit gives us the wisdom to understand God and know Him better as we grow in our relationship with Him. 1 Corinthians 2:10 says, "But it was to us that God revealed these things by his Spirit. For his Spirit searches out everything and shows us God's deep secrets." Having true, intimate knowledge of God is the only way we can ever understand His ways and our purpose here on earth; therefore, we must develop and maintain a close relationship with the Holy Spirit who is our source of spiritual wisdom.

Knowing and understanding the Word of God is vitally important to our Christian walk, but we cannot come to a divine understanding without the Holy Spirit. Regardless of a person's reading level, extensive vocabulary, or understanding of complex ideas, no one can truly understand God's Word without the help of the Holy Spirit. The Bible explains that "the natural person does not accept the things of the Spirit of God, for they are folly to him, and he is not able to understand them because they are spiritually discerned" (1 Cor. 2:14).

Sure, we may understand parts of a story or understand the roles of certain characters mentioned in the Bible, but without the Holy Spirit enlightening our understanding, we cannot comprehend the eternal value and application of God's Word for our personal lives. Because of the Holy Spirit's power in helping people understand the Bible, you and I can read the exact same scripture only to have completely different meanings. We may even have opposing emotions that leave one of us rejoicing while the other is brought to tears. When we let the Holy Spirit guide our understanding of the Bible, we will experience knowledge far beyond anything the world could ever teach.

The Holy Spirit also helps us to know our purpose and calling in life. Every Believer has the same purpose: Know God and make Him known. These two things are the key elements of discipleship. 2 Timothy 1:9 says, "For God saved us and called us to live a holy life. He did this, not because we deserved it, but because that was his plan from before the beginning of time—to show us his grace through Christ Jesus." We are called to live a holy life because that has been

God's plan from the beginning. Only through holiness can we draw near to Him and know Him. When we live a holy life through the power of the Holy Spirit, we can make Him known to the world. In Matthew 28:18-20, Jesus said, "Go therefore and make disciples of all nations, baptizing them in the name of the Father and of the Son and of the Holy Spirit, teaching them to observe all that I have commanded you. And behold, I am with you always, to the end of the age." While our ultimate purpose of living a holy life that glorifies God is clear, our calling is not always as evident.

WALKING IN PURPOSE

The specific calling God has for a person's life will facilitate their purpose of knowing God and making Him known. Many people confuse their calling with their career, but the two are not always the same. A job is what you get *paid* to do, but a calling is what you were *made* to do. *Vocation* comes from the Latin word *vocare*, which means "to call." In perfect circumstances every believer would work in a career field that aligns with their calling, but sadly, that is not the case. People all over the world spend their lives working a job that doesn't bring them any sense of fulfillment or significance. But let me hasten to say that meaning matters more than money. Anyone can make a dollar, but it takes a special person to make a difference. If your main concern is money, you will never make enough and will always be miserable deep down in your soul.

Living out the calling that God has for your life will bring you satisfaction and give God glory. However, not living out your calling will always leave you hungry and desperate for more. I have learned that proper people placement prevents problems, and poor people placement promotes problems. When you rely on the Holy Spirit to help direct your path to the place in which you were created to be, He will reveal to you all that God has planned for your life. Now, He most likely won't reveal it all at once, but through a daily

When you rely on the Holy Spirit to help direct your path to the place in which you were created to be, He will reveal to you all that God has planned for your life.

relationship with the Holy Spirit, you will come to see all that God is doing and wants to do in and through you.

A few good indicators to help you know if you're not living out the calling God has for your life are frustration, fatigue, and failure. Your calling will not leave you feeling frustrated constantly and it won't leave you feeling burnt out and exhausted. Also, if you continually experience failure in what you are doing, it's an indicator you aren't living out your calling.

Three good indicators that you *are* living out your calling can be that you are focused, fulfilled, and fruitful. When you are working and serving in the places God created you to be, you will know beyond a shadow of a doubt that you're doing exactly what you're meant to do and you will experience the greatest fulfillment. Also, when you are fulfilling your purpose, you will experience success and significance, because where God guides, He provides.

As I studied the life of Jesus, I realized the importance of His first recorded words in the Bible. In Luke 2, Mary and Joseph were on the way home from Jerusalem after Passover when they noticed that Jesus was not with them. They immediately turned back to find Him, but they searched for three days before finding Him in the temple. Could you imagine thinking that you had lost the Son of God? I would have been worried sick!

Like any distraught parent would do, Mary (probably raising her voice) questioned Jesus about his actions and let Him know that they had been frantically searching for Him for days. In verse 2, Jesus (with a calm and direct voice) speaks His first recorded words in scripture: "Why did you seek Me? Did you not know that I must be about My Father's business?"

In contrast to His first words, Jesus' last words before dying on the cross were, "It is finished" (John 19:30). From His first recorded words to His last, Jesus was always about

God's business. His only focus was fulfilling His purpose on earth to reconcile us all with God. Just as Jesus was here to do God's business, you and I were created for a unique purpose and placed on this earth to do the business God has for us. We can't be content with salvation and nothing more. We must strive for closeness with the Holy Spirit and allow Him to help us know God deeply, understand His Word so that it can guide our lives, and seek to fulfill our divine purpose.

CEASE TO COMPARE

We have all heard the saying "Comparison is the thief of joy," and we usually agree that the quote is true. However, we still find ourselves comparing so many things in our lives to what we see around us or on social media. It is crazy how we can find something so wonderful and special at one point, but after comparing it to something else, we no longer have the same perspective or see the same worth in what we previously valued.

In Galatians 6:4–5, God teaches a valuable lesson about comparison when saying, "Pay careful attention to your own work, for then you will get the satisfaction of a job well done, and you won't need to compare yourself to anyone else. For we are each responsible for our own conduct." Just as we can have as much of God as we want, we can be used by God as much as we allow Him to use us. I've often said that you don't have to pray, "God, use me"; just get usable, and He will wear you out!

The disciples were the closest to Jesus, yet they still struggled with comparison. In Luke 22, Jesus spends His last meal with his disciples before going to the cross. He pours out His heart about future betrayal and how "it has been determined that the Son of Man must die" (v. 22). In all the seriousness of the moment and the heartbreaking reality that the Lord was facing, verse 24 says that the disciples "began to argue among themselves about who would be the greatest among them." Comparison stole their last moments with their Savior.

In the gospel of John, the author (John) refers to himself as "the disciple Jesus loved" at least five different times. John also compared himself to Peter when detailing the winner of a foot-race to the empty tomb. In John 20:3-4, he writes, "Peter and the other disciple started out for the tomb. They were both running, but the other disciple outran Peter and reached the tomb first." Again, in verse 8, John makes it clear: "Then the disciple who had reached the tomb first also went in, and he saw and believed." John's comparison of himself to Peter makes it seem as if he was more concerned about the race than the resurrection.

You see, comparison will always compromise your perspective and cripple your calling. You won't be able to fulfill the calling on your life when you're busy comparing it to someone else's. There is no substitute for you. No one else was created to do what God has for you, and you will never be fulfilled trying to live out someone else's calling. Trying to walk in a calling that isn't for you is like trying to walk in a shoe that doesn't fit, it will be uncomfortable and you won't get as far as you could if you were to walk in what fits you best.

You won't be able to fulfill the calling on your life when you're busy comparing it to someone else's. There is no substitute for you.

Ephesians 2:10 says, "For we are God's masterpiece. He has created us anew in Christ Jesus, so we can do the good things he planned for us long ago." While your calling may be new to you, it isn't new to God. The whole reason you were created is to fulfill a specific purpose. God didn't create you and then decide on your calling. Scripture is clear that you were created specifically for a calling that He planned long before you were ever born.

The word "masterpiece" in verse 10 is the Greek word *poiēma*, from which we get the English word *poem*.[1] A poem is defined as a composition that is characterized by great beauty of expression. Just as a poem is carefully crafted by its author to evoke great beauty and deep meaning through precise expression, you were carefully and thoughtfully created by the God of the universe to fulfill an eternal purpose through a precise calling. Don't let comparison steal your joy and cripple your calling. Instead, let the Holy Spirit guide you into a divine understanding of what you were created to do.

There is no calling that is superior to another. Being in full-time ministry doesn't mean someone has a greater calling than anyone else. If you are doing what you are called to do, and I'm doing what I am called to do, then we will both be fulfilled because we are doing what pleases God and brings Him glory!

The Holy Spirit is your helper, and He wants to lead you every step of the way in the divine direction that God has planned for your life. But to walk confidently and faithfully in all that you were created to do, you must seek divine wisdom and avoid destination disease.

SEEK DIVINE WISDOM

Knowing your calling and living out your calling are two different things. I know that I am called to preach, however, to live out that calling daily, I have to rely on the Holy Spirit to guide me in knowing what to specifically preach at every event and in every service, how to best minister to those in our congregation, and how to lead my staff and others who seek my advice. I must dedicate time to spend with the Holy Spirit in order to gain divine wisdom and direction in how I should live out my calling each day.

The same is true for your life and calling. If you don't know exactly what your calling is in life, you must prioritize spiritual disciplines such as prayer and Bible study. Ask the Holy Spirit to help you know the right direction you should be going and what specific things you should be doing to serve God with your life. If what you are doing or want to do does not align with God's Word, that is a good indicator that it's not what you should pursue. If you are not sure what you should be praying, commit what you are currently doing to the Lord and pray that He shows you stop signs if it's not the right direction.

Romans 8:26–27 explains the role the Holy Spirit has in helping us to know God's will:

> And the Holy Spirit helps us in our weakness. For example, we don't know what God wants us to pray for. But the Holy Spirit prays for us with groanings that cannot be expressed in words. And the Father who knows all hearts knows what the Spirit is saying, for the Spirit pleads for us believers in harmony with God's own will.

Our greatest desire should be to live in harmony with God's will, and the Holy Spirit is our only source for gaining the wisdom we lack to make decisions concerning our calling. When you spend time with Him in prayer and dig into God's Word, you will gain confidence in the knowledge you have of God's plan for your life.

When I first started pastoring Sweeten Hill Church, I worked forty hours a week in a machine shop to be able to provide for my family. In those days and in our area, there weren't any full-time pastors, they all worked a second job to make ends meet. But I truly believed that God had so much more for me and for our congregation of thirty or so people. I just knew that I was going to accomplish much because I knew that I served an all-powerful God who could "accomplish infinitely more than we might ask or think" (Eph. 3:20).

I felt the Lord leading me to step out in faith, and the more I prayed and dug into God's Word, the more He confirmed in my heart that I was to trust Him for more. So, I left my job at the machine shop to be the only full-time pastor anyone in our area had ever known. As I stepped out in faith and gave God full control of my time, my finances, and my ministry, He began to do more within our little church than I could've ever imagined. We started growing like never before, and within a few short years, we had over three hundred members.

Leaving my job at the machine shop made no sense to anyone, but your calling will always be unexplainable outside of the Holy Spirit. Only when you seek the Holy Spirit for divine wisdom and truly submit everything in your life to Him will the unexplainable begin to happen. God doesn't want you to be confused or ignorant concerning your calling. Ephesians 1:18 says, "I pray that your hearts will be flooded with light so that you can understand the confident hope he has given to those he called—his holy people who are his rich and glorious inheritance."

God wants you to understand and be confident in the calling He has placed on your life!

You need divine wisdom for *today* in order to experience true fulfillment. Maybe you are called to the nursing field to care for and minister to people in a hospital. Sure, you may be confident in knowing your calling, but only through the Holy Spirit guiding your life each day can you know what to say and do with everyone you come into contact with each day. If you will truly seek His wisdom and direction, He will give you words at just the right time to stir in someone's heart or to open their eyes to the gospel.

Maybe you are a teacher who knows that you are doing what you were called to do, but with the help of the Holy Spirit, you will have an awareness of needs beyond academic content. The Holy Spirit will nudge you to share specific encouragement, speak truth, and even notice needs at just the right moments throughout your day.

Hebrews 3:7 says, "*Today* when you hear his voice" (emphasis added), which means the Lord has something specific for you each day, and only through spending time with Him and maintaining a close relationship with Him can you have the divine wisdom you need to live out the specific assignments of your calling each day.

AVOID DESTINATION DISEASE

When it comes to living out your calling, it can be easy to plan ahead and determine the best time to really start living for God in a more committed way. If you aren't careful, "someday" will never arrive and you will have wasted a lot time procrastinating. There will be no better time to truly live for the Lord than right now.

I can remember when Savannah Abigail was a newborn, and Barbara and I would say that we couldn't wait until she was sleeping through the night. As she got older, we couldn't wait to see her walking, then out of diapers, and even able to get herself ready. We didn't want to wish her life away but we were so excited to celebrate all the new milestones. Before we knew it, she had graduated from every milestone of childhood right through high school and into college. We would lay beside each other in the bed and night as empty nesters and talk about how we would give anything to hear little footsteps run into our room in the middle of the night just one more time.

Just as Savannah was grown in the blink of an eye, your opportunities to live out your calling fly by just as quickly. Without even realizing it, ten years will have passed without you ever stepping out in faith. You'll look back and remember all of the "if..., then..." statements you made that never turned into action.

God wants you to walk in your purpose through the power of the Holy Spirit right where you are. Don't diminish where you are by hoping and waiting for what's next. There is work to be done for God's Kingdom in your home, at your job, and in this season of your life. Waiting for what is next only means you are wasting what is now.

The enemy wants you to believe that you need to wait until you are more of something before God can *really* use your life. You may find yourself saying things such as, "I'm just a _____, so my calling isn't important right now," or, "If I can get _____, I'll be able to live out my calling." Both of those statements are lies of the enemy. You are right where God wants you to be because if He wanted you somewhere, guess what— He's powerful enough to move you!

You may be a small business owner thinking that you need to achieve more financial success before you can really walk in your calling, but it might not be about the business you build but the employees you inspire. Maybe you are a stay-at-home mom who thinks you will fulfill your purpose by going back to work once the kids are grown, but your calling may not be tied to the check you receive but the children you raise. Don't minimize your current influence by thinking your future holds opportunities for greater impact.

There will certainly be more maintenance days than magnificent days as you walk in your calling. There will probably be a lot of discouraging days mixed in with the encouraging days. Neither of the previous statements reflects the importance of your specific calling in your current season. The next level will be full of maintenance days and discouraging days as well because those are what keep us reliant on God. You will only be sustained in every season through purpose and Holy Spirit calling.

I pray that you will diligently seek the Lord in knowing your true calling. Fulfillment is found in complete surrender because you can only know God and make Him known in your life through a close relationship with the Holy Spirit. You're not meant to wonder or question your calling. I hope you know that you know that you know exactly why you were created, and walk confidently as the chosen, called, and gifted child of God that you are. With the Holy Spirit's help, you can wake up every day knowing beyond a shadow of a doubt that you are doing exactly what God created you to do!

TIME TO REFLECT

- When you get to know God intimately and understand scripture, you see God as a good father and see yourself as the child He adores. Read Galatians 4:6. He wants us to cry out to Him calling Him Father. How does that affect the way you relate to God? Why might you or others have a hard time thinking about God as Father?

- Television and social media constantly inform us of what everyone else is doing. Why do you think we are fascinated by everyone else's circumstances? How does that effect our perspective? In which areas of your life are you most tempted to compare your situation to someone else's?

- There is nothing wrong with setting goals and having big dreams, but God doesn't want us catching destination disease. Why can it be so hard to avoid desiring what's next? How has that kept you from making the most of the current moment or season? What can you do to prevent destination disease?

CHAPTER 11
MISSION READY

SINCE I WAS a young man, I have tried to learn from those who have been where I haven't been and have gone where I would like to go. I love to sit down with great leaders and businessmen to ask questions about their successes and even their failures in life. I've always thought it wise to learn from the experiences of others as much as I can.

Years ago I got on a plane to Oklahoma City, Oklahoma, to meet David Green, founder of Hobby Lobby. It was such a tremendous opportunity because I was able to spend some time with Mr. Green and ask him questions about his background, spiritual life, and great success. I was interested to learn about his upbringing and how he came to open Hobby Lobby.

Mr. Green told me that his father and mother pastored churches all his life. He had five siblings, who all were either pastors or married to pastors. Everyone in his family was involved in full-time ministry in one way or another, so he felt incredible pressure to go into ministry himself. But it wasn't what he felt called to do. His experience working at a five-and-dime store caused him to develop a love for retail. He was intrigued with the idea of buying something for ten cents and selling it for twenty cents.

In 1970, Mr. Green and his wife, Barbara, took out a loan for six hundred dollars to purchase a framing machine to start making miniature picture frames. Their business continued to grow into the great success that Hobby Lobby is today. Mr. Green said biblical principles have always been the foundation of his business. Even with over nine hundred stores and over forty-three thousand employees, he continues to value people over profits. Not only are his stores closed on Sundays for his employees to spend time with their families, but 50 percent of all proceeds go to support ministry. He may not have gone into ministry like the rest of his family members, but he followed the calling God placed on his life and used the gifts God gave him to fund family ministries for many years.

Just as God had a specific purpose for David Green's life, every person has a specific calling on his or her life. You can be sure that when God appoints you, He anoints you. Where God guides, He provides. When it comes to the calling on all of our lives, the Holy Spirit gives supernatural wisdom, ability, stamina, and protection for us to do His will. We can't accomplish anything of significance without the power of the Holy Spirit in our lives, because nothing in our own strength or ability will last.

DIVINELY GIFTED

Corrie Ten Boom said, "The human spirit fails except when the Holy Spirit fills," and I'm so thankful that He not only fills us but He imparts special abilities to us. When we accept Jesus Christ as Savior, the Holy Spirit comes into our lives and brings gifts! God made you a unique person and put within you a unique passion, because you were created for a unique purpose. So many people spend their entire lives never knowing why they were put on this earth, but God does not want you to live in the dark about your specific calling and your divine giftedness.

The Bible tells us there are three things we should not be ignorant concerning: the second coming of Christ (1 Thess. 4:13–18), the devices of the devil (2 Cor. 2:11), and our spiritual gifts (1 Cor. 12:1). Life is so important, and it's vital that we know how the Holy Spirit has specifically gifted us. First Corinthians 12:13 says, "The human body has many parts, but the many parts make up one whole body. So it is with the body of Christ." Verse 27 says, "All of you together are Christ's body, and each of you is a part of it." Therefore, just as the parts of a human body work together to ensure optimum health and functioning, every person in the body of Christ must use their spiritual gifts to ensure God's perfect will is done here on earth.

It's vital that we know how the Holy Spirit has specifically gifted us.

The Bible describes us all as mere "jars of clay" (2 Cor. 4:7). We're cracked pots. Every one of us has flaws and weaknesses because of our flesh. Paul urges us, in Philippians 3, to "rely on what Christ Jesus has done for us" and "put no confidence in human effort" (v. 3). Our only abilities are because of the Holy Spirit within us, and our spiritual gifts are given and guided by Him alone.

Before we talk about what spiritual gifts are, let's first understand what they're not. Spiritual gifts should not be confused with natural talents or abilities. When you were born, there are certain natural abilities that are a part of your DNA. Some people are born with a talent for working with their hands, others may be really good at cooking, and some may be great at dancing. Many times the natural talents and abilities a person has can usually be seen in other family members as well. Talent is what you have when you are born, but a spiritual gift is what you get when you are born again.

For example, I've always wished that I could sing because there have been so many times in my years of preaching that a song has come to my mind in the middle of my sermon and I've wanted to burst into song and lead the congregation in worship. Now if you have ever heard me sing, you will be glad I don't give into that desire! I sing good but I sound bad! When it comes to my natural singing ability, I'm somewhere between bad and terrible. I just wasn't born with that talent, and I'm ok with that. Some people were not born with the ability to sing, but no one has ever been honest with them about how they really sound. And every season of American Idol has a special segment to highlight those people!

Spiritual gifts also should not be confused with the fruit of the Spirit. While the fruit of the Spirit develops after receiving the Holy Spirit at salvation, the fruit of the Spirit is characteristics that develop within you over time as a result of the Holy Spirit dwelling within you and changing you from the inside out. The fruit of the Spirit is not unique or specific to each person but available to all believers alike.

Spiritual gifts are special, specific attributes given by the Spirit to every member of the body to use within the context of the body. The Holy Spirit equips the called and gives spiritual gifts for the calling. 1 Corinthians 12:11 says, "It is the one and only Spirit who distributes all these gifts. He alone decides which gift each person should have." When the Holy Spirit comes, He brings at least one but usually multiple gifts for you to use within the body of Christ to further God's Kingdom. While you may receive more than one gift, you won't receive them all.

Spiritual gifts are unique to each believer, and your spiritual gifts have an eternal purpose! When I was a young boy,

I was terrified to speak in front of people. Even when people came over to our house, my mama said that I would always run to my room and hide under my bed. If people came up to us in public to talk, I would hide behind my mother to keep from having to talk to anyone. As a student, I refused to stand in front of the class to give any kind of oral report. Every time the teacher assigned a speaking assignment, I took a zero instead of standing in front of the class. It's safe to say that I was not born with a talent for public speaking, but after getting saved, the Holy Spirit gave me the gift of preaching.

Since my salvation experience, I have had a burden for lost people and have been willing to go out of my way to clearly and effectively communicate the gospel to anyone who will listen. I no longer have a fear of speaking, not because of anything about my own strength, but because the unlimited power of the Holy Spirit lives inside of me and gives me the ability and desire to share Jesus with others! Whether I'm in front of ten or ten thousand people, I enjoy every opportunity I get to share the gospel. When the Holy Spirit gave me the gift of preaching, He replaced my insecurity and fear with godly confidence that only comes from Him!

You must understand and accept that spiritual gifts are given for two very specific reasons. First Peter 4:10 says, "God has given each of you a gift from his great variety of spiritual gifts. Use them well to serve one another"; therefore, your gifts are never meant to be self-serving. Verse 11 also says, "Do it with all the strength and energy that God supplies. Then everything you do will bring glory to God through Jesus Christ," which means that your gifts should also glorify God. Spiritual gifts should be used for advancing God's kingdom through the building up of others and magnifying the name of Jesus!

Maybe you have a hard time believing that you have a spiritual gift because you just don't recognize any special, specific attributes, but let me quickly remind you of what the beginning of 1 Peter 4:10 clearly says, "God has given *each of you* a gift from his great variety of spiritual gifts" (emphasis added). Whether you recognize or understand your giftedness or not, the Bible makes it clear that you have a spiritual gift.

UNDERSTANDING IS VITAL

Having a good understanding of what the Bible says about the different kinds of spiritual gifts will help you to identify and accurately use the gift(s) the Holy Spirit has given you. Scholars and theologians have debated over the exact number of spiritual gifts, depending on which person or spiritual gifts test you refer to; you could find reasoning for anywhere between thirteen and twenty-three spiritual gifts. The Book of 1 Corinthians lists thirteen spiritual gifts, the Book of Romans lists four more, and then there are six other considerations from various books in the Bible. I'm not here to tell you exactly how many spiritual gifts there are, I'm more concerned with you digging into God's Word and discovering your giftedness through your own learning experience with the Lord.

Regardless of the debate over exactly how many gifts are mentioned in scripture, spiritual gifts are commonly broken down into three categories: ministry gifts, motivational gifts, and manifestation gifts.

Ministry gifts are seen as tools used for building up the church. Ephesians 4:11 says, "Now these are the gifts Christ gave to the church: the apostles, the prophets, the evangelists, and the pastors and teachers." Verse 12 explains the purpose of these gifts: "Their responsibility is to equip God's people to do his work and build up the church, the body of Christ." These gifts are a calling to specific offices or positions in the church in which no one can place themselves. The main goal of those whom God has gifted and called to these positions should be to equip God's people for acts of service.

Motivational gifts are seen as more practical in nature, and they reveal God's personality through His people. Examples of commonly agreed-upon motivational gifts are serving, mercy, giving, encouragement, hospitality, and administration. Romans 12:6–8 says, "If your gift is prophesying, then prophesy in accordance with your faith; if it is serving, then serve; if it is teaching, then teach; if it is to encourage, then give encouragement; if it is giving, then give generously; if it is to lead, do it diligently; if it is to show mercy, do it cheerfully" (NIV). These gifts are often seen as shaping the inner motivation of a believer to serve within the body of Christ.

Manifestation gifts, also called miraculous gifts, are seen as supernatural in nature and reveal God's power among His people. Examples of common manifestation gifts are healing, miracles, speaking in tongues, interpretation of tongues, and discernment. First Corinthians 12:7–10 (NIV) says,

> Now to each one the manifestation of the Spirit is given for the common good. To one there is given through the Spirit a message of wisdom, to another a message of knowledge by means of the same Spirit, to another faith by the same Spirit, to another gifts of healing by that one Spirit, to another miraculous powers, to another prophecy, to another distinguishing between spirits, to another speaking in different kinds of tongues, and to still another the interpretation of tongues.

Many Christians would probably say that manifestation gifts such as healing, miracles, or even prophecy were more common in biblical times than they are today. Manifestation gifts were more prominent in Jesus' day because the manifestation of the Holy Spirit's power validated that what they were saying agreed with God, but we have a completed Bible that we are able to use as validation of what God says against what is spoken and preached.

If you take into consideration the different types of gifts mentioned previously and still have no idea or indication as to what your spiritual gift might be, I suggest you take a spiritual gifts test. You can find a link to a free spiritual gifts test in the appendix of this book. I hope you will take the test and really dive into understanding how God wants you to use your gift for His kingdom!

There are many great rewards for understanding your spiritual gift and using it for the Lord. When you know your giftedness, it will help clarify what God's will is for your life. You will gain a better perspective and be able to filter opportunities and circumstances through the lens of your spiritual gift. It will produce great significance in your life when you truly know what you were specifically created to do and then walk in that calling on your life.

You will also be able to use your gift to benefit others and glorify God. The Holy Spirit will lead you into circumstances that you may have never thought possible just so you can help someone else and give God all the credit. If you will seek the Holy Spirit for fresh anointings of His power, He will use you in the most incredible and unexplainable ways.

I can remember sitting in my office one Monday afternoon. All of our pastors are off on Mondays, so I knew it would be really quiet in the office for me to get a lot of studying done for my sermon. A little before two in the afternoon, I had this overwhelming feeling that I needed to take something out to my vehicle. I thought to myself that it could wait, but something or someone kept saying to me that I needed to go out to my vehicle right at that moment.

As I walked to my vehicle, I got on my phone to call someone for their birthday, but I noticed a young man standing by himself near the corner of the church. As I walked towards him, he asked if he could talk with me. I said, "Yes, let me finish up with this phone call and I will talk with you." I put my phone away and asked him how he was doing. He said, "I'm not doing well at all. I've lost my home because my wife wants a divorce. She's leaving me." I told him how sorry I was to hear that he was going through such a difficult time.

This life is too important to wonder and wander any longer without using everything the Holy Spirit has given you to fight the good fight and experience victory in every circumstance.

I asked where his wife was, and he said, "She's on her way here. She's been seeing a counselor here and is coming to tell the counselor that she's made up her mind to leave me for good." I prayed over him and then asked if I could meet his wife. When she arrived, I introduced myself and offered to walk with them to the counseling office. The room was dark when we walked in, so I decided to sit with them until the counselor arrived. As I talked with the couple, I learned about the different struggles the husband had in their marriage. I learned about how the wife was tired of him not getting any better or staying committed to change. After some time, I was able to connect them with a couple in our church whose gift is shepherding and teaching other couples in marriage. The wife was willing to try again as long as the husband would remain accountable.

I'm happy to report that the young married couple on the edge of divorce that day have worked through their issues and are stronger than they've ever been. I don't share this story to brag on anything I've done, because it had nothing at all to do with me. I'm a terrible counselor. The Holy Spirit is the One who led me to that couple and gave me the precise words for that circumstance. The Holy Spirit gifted me with a burden for people who are hurting. Another part of my giftedness is pastoring people. Only by the power of the Holy Spirit can I have anything to say or offer anyone in need. And I've realized that there is so much significance in helping others, because when people grow stronger in their walk with Christ, He gets all the glory and His kingdom grows all the more!

When you understand your spiritual giftedness, it will make your calling and purpose clear. This life is too important to wonder and wander any longer without using everything the Holy Spirit has given you to fight the good fight and experience victory in every circumstance. It is vitally important to the kingdom of God that you find the right position and regularly use your spiritual gifts.

RIGHT POSITION

Years ago there was a baseball player named Dale Murphy who came up as a hind catcher, but his only problem was that when someone tried to steal second base, he would throw the ball over the second baseman's head into center field. His coaches decided he wasn't going to make it as a hind catcher, so they put him at first base. He didn't do too well at first base either. Finally, they put Dale Murphy in center field and he started winning Gold Glove awards.

The key to Dale's success was that he got into the right place. He wasn't reaching his full potential at the other positions because they were not the right place for him. The same is true for our spiritual life when it comes to our giftedness. When you understand what the Holy Spirit has gifted you to do, you will get in the right position and become excellent at the specific purpose God has for you. Only through the power of the Holy Spirit living out your giftedness through you can you experience success and significance for God!

When considering your spiritual gift and being in the right position, you'll want to ask yourself if you desire it and if you are good at it. If the Holy Spirit has truly given you a certain spiritual gift, you will enjoy doing it and look forward to doing it. You will also be good at whatever your giftedness is. Proverbs 18:16 says, "A man's gift makes room for him and brings him before the great," which means a person is known for their giftedness. Your spiritual gifts will open doors for you to do things that you otherwise couldn't do.

There was an older man in our church who wanted to get more involved, so he sought out an opportunity to serve. His wife and two grown daughters all served in children's ministry and he knew they could always use extra help, so he started volunteering in kids' church on Sunday mornings. One afternoon, he sat around the dinner table with his family and started talking about how bad the kids were in the children's ministry. Everyone was shocked by what he was saying and wondered why he thought the kids were so bad. He explained, "They run around everywhere when we take them to the indoor playground. They are always screaming and chasing each other. In the auditorium, they jump around during worship. They always get up during the service to get water or go to the bathroom. They are just nonstop, and the way they behave is ridiculous."

One of his children spoke up and said, "Dad, it sounds to me like they are just being kids! They're not terrible, they seem completely normal." As they continued eating, the man's family began to ask him if he ever enjoyed serving in the children's ministry and if he looked forward to it on Sunday mornings. He said, "No, I'm just going to quit serving." His oldest son had listened to everything being said and finally spoke up, "Dad, I just think you're in the wrong seat on the bus. If you get in the right seat, you'll enjoy the ride much more." You see, the man was serving to fill what he thought was a needed position, not out of the desire of his heart.

Within a few short weeks that same man got involved with a men's ministry group that builds wheelchair ramps and completes house repairs for elderly people, widows, and needy families. He is gifted to work with his hands and help people in need, therefore, he needed to be involved in service projects, not kid's church. Now that he is in the right seat on the bus, he definitely enjoys the ride! He is always volunteering to build sets, displays, photo walls, and any other projects that are needed around the church in addition to helping the men's group with projects. He looks forward to serving and enjoys every moment of it!

If you find yourself saying, "I love to entertain," then maybe you have the spiritual gift of hospitality. Maybe you love being very generous to others, then your gift may be giving. If other people would describe you as a great cheerleader for people, then you may have the spiritual gift of encouragement. Think about what you are good at and what you enjoy doing, but also consider what others recognize in you as well. These are all ways to help you gain a better perspective of how the Holy Spirit has gifted you.

Don't simply signup for whatever is needed within your church or community just because you want to serve. If you serve where you are not gifted, you will constantly be frustrated or unsatisfied, and you will want to quit. But when you begin serving in the areas God has gifted you, serving will become a source of joy in your life and you will have a greater feeling of significance than you ever have before.

REGULAR USAGE

Just as there are benefits to knowing and using your spiritual gift, there are also ramifications for neglecting and not developing your spiritual gifts. First Timothy 4:14 says, "Do not neglect the spiritual gift you received through the prophecy spoken over you when the elders of the church laid their hands on you." The Holy Spirit has given you specific gifts for a specific reason, and it is a very serious thing to God if you don't use the gifts you've been given.

According to Matthew 25, the Parable of the Talents, not using what is given to you has great consequences.

According to Matthew 25, the Parable of the Talents, not using what is given to you has great consequences. Of the three men who received talents in the parable, only two of them used their talents and multiplied them. The one man who didn't use his talent ended up losing everything. He was fearful of the outcome, so he chose instead to play it safe.

Oftentimes, we don't develop our gifts out of fear. Maybe you aren't sure how you are supposed to use your gift, so you do nothing at all. Others may focus too much on wanting certain gifts that others have and miss out on developing and using their own. Regardless of what keeps a person from using their spiritual gifts, the Bible is clear that they are not to be neglected.

Matthew 25:28–29 says, "So take the talent from him and give it to him who has the ten talents. For to everyone who has will more be given, and he will have an abundance. But from the one who has not, even what he has will be taken away." When it comes to the spiritual giftedness that the Holy Spirit has given you, if you don't use it, you lose it.

The Bible is also clear that it isn't just enough to have gifts but to maximize every opportunity you are given to use your gifts for God. Second Timothy 1:6 says, "This is why I remind you to fan into flames the spiritual gift God gave you when I laid my hands on you," which means you must stir up the gifts you've been given. Don't become complacent in using your gifts or grow accustomed to being gifted by the Holy Spirit. You must fan the flame and see every opportunity to use your gift as a divine assignment from God.

Humility is a great way to fan the flame of your spiritual gift because how you use your giftedness should always and only be to glorify God and help others. Be careful that you do not become prideful of the abilities given to you by the Holy Spirit. If you have been gifted to speak, make sure you use your voice to share the gospel and promote Jesus above yourself. If you have been gifted with teaching, words of wisdom, or knowledge, be sure that you do not grow confident in thinking that you are wise, knowledgeable, or talented in your own strength. For those who are gifted in leadership, you must be sure that you always lead from a biblical foundation and reflect Jesus in your leadership.

Spiritual gifts should never be used to build a platform for oneself. We live in a social media-driven world where it is so easy to get caught up in likes, comments, and views. People may recognize your giftedness and compliment you often, but always be sure to redirect that praise to God. When we accept praise from others without acknowledging God as our source, pride will begin to build in our hearts. God will not share His glory with anyone. Make sure that you do not become more focused on gaining favor in the eyes of the world than pleasing the audience of One.

The enemy would love more for you to grow slack in fanning the flame of your spiritual gift so that he can whisper lies and deceit in your ear. You must be vigilant to praise God in everything you are able to accomplish for Him because whatever you don't turn to praise will turn to pride. Becoming prideful of your spiritual giftedness can lead to you losing the gift just as the man in the parable lost his. It's not just about using the gift but using the gift correctly. The use of your gift must always have an eternal impact and a kingdom perspective.

The Holy Spirit has fully equipped you for successfully fulfilling the calling God has placed on your life, but it is your responsibility to make the most out of every opportunity. No one is saved to sit. We're all saved to serve, and when you regularly use your gifts and seek ways to fan the flame, the opportunities to impact God's kingdom will multiply just as the talents did with the men in the parable. God is the God of abundance, and He will maximize everything you surrender to Him!

Never forget that you were created on purpose for an unlimited purpose! When you seek closeness with the Holy Spirit and completely surrender to His plans, He will equip you and call you to the most exciting journey you could ever take in this life. He has the greatest plans for you, but don't forget that when He calls you and blesses you, He has more than you in mind. You are a vital part of the body of Christ! Step into your giftedness because you are well equipped and mission ready!

TIME TO REFLECT

- How does it make you feel to know that you are divinely gifted by the Holy Spirit for a unique purpose? Do you feel a greater sense of responsibility for how you live your life when you better understand spiritual gifts?

- When considering the three categories for spiritual gifts, do any of the three stick out to you the most concerning your own spiritual giftedness? If so or if you already know your spiritual gift(s), what areas of your life could you be more intentional about using your gifts?

- Why do you think in today's world it can be easy to not use or develop a spiritual gift out of fear? What kind of obstacles get in the way of you using your gifts? Are there certain circumstances in your own life where you might be reluctant to use your spiritual gift?

CHAPTER 12
MIRACULOUS WORKS

THERE IS NO question about it, God is still in the miracle-working business. He has allowed me to witness and be a part of so many miraculous circumstances throughout my Christian walk. From early in my ministry, God chose to lift my faith through the miraculous healing of my wife, Barbara. The Mayo Clinic said that she would live the rest of her life having multiple seizures a day, but she prayed and believed that God was going to heal her. I wish I could say that I had her same faith, but God used Barbara's healing to teach me to believe Him for great miracles.

In my years of pastoring Rock Springs Church, I have seen God perform miracles in the lives of our members as well as in the growth of our church. I remember a young couple in our church that was expecting their second child, a baby boy. They had received concerning news after an ultrasound that their baby was showing strong signs of being born with Down syndrome. The common indicators were present in the ultrasound images, and the doctor was sure of the diagnosis. The couple, however, believed Psalm 139:13: "You made all the delicate, inner parts of my body and knit me together in my mother's womb" (NLT). They knew only the Creator could determine the outcome, and they believed Him for a different diagnosis.

After hearing the news from the couple, I committed to pray for them daily, but one Sunday morning at the end of our service, I felt the Holy Spirit led me to pray corporately for the couple and their baby. They came to the altar, and many people came to lay hands on them and pray. Even after praying, I felt the Holy Spirit prompt me once again to challenge our congregation to commit to praying and fasting for that precious baby each day until the next ultrasound. As I called out days, hands of commitment went up all across the sanctuary. For thirty days, multiple people were praying and fasting in the belief that God was going to heal that baby boy.

On the day of the ultrasound, thousands prayed during the ultrasound. To this day I can remember getting a call from that father with the report that the ultrasound showed no signs or indications of autism or any other issue. The doctors couldn't explain what they saw, but the couple knew exactly what had happened. God performed a miracle! But I'm so thankful that God did an even greater miracle when that precious boy gave His life to Christ!

God worked another incredible miracle experience in our church concerning other couples having babies as well. At the end of another Sunday service, the Holy Spirit prompted me once again to pray for couples who were struggling to have a baby. It's not as if the sermon had related to infertility in any way, but the Holy Spirit told me to invite couples down to the altar for prayer. I gave the invitation and twenty couples came forward for prayer. Again, members of our congregation came forward to lay hands on each couple as we corporately prayed for God to bless each couple with a baby.

After the service, I wrote the names of all twenty couples on a sheet of paper and committed to praying over that list daily. Every morning during my quiet time with the Lord, I would take that sheet of paper and call out the names of each couple as I asked God to them with a baby. I never asked that God give them children in any specific way but that He would just provide.

I'm so happy to report to you that our church family has been rejoicing year after year as couples report how God has blessed their families with children! Some of the couples were told they couldn't have children due to certain issues, but God provided. Other couples had tried for years with no success and no answers as to why they couldn't get pregnant, but God provided. God provided children to several couples through adoption. There were a few couples who wanted prayer for the adoption process and ended up pregnant. After the ultrasound showed twins, one couple told me I could quit praying!

HE HASN'T CHANGED

God has shown up in so many miraculous ways over the years because He is a miracle-working God. Hebrews 13:8 confirms that "Jesus Christ is the same yesterday, today, and forever." We can expect Him to be Who He's always been and do what He's always done. I've learned that most Believers don't have a problem with yesterday. They confidently believe that over two thousand years ago Jesus shed His blood on the cross and it washes away our sins today.

Most Believers don't have a problem with forever either. They have no problem believing 1 Thessalonians 4:16–17:

> For the Lord himself will come down from heaven with
> a commanding shout, with the voice of the archangel,
> and with the trumpet call of God. First, the believers
> who have died will rise from their graves. Then, together
> with them, we who are still alive and remain on the

earth will be caught up in the clouds to meet the Lord in the air. Then we will be with the Lord forever.

We're all in agreement that the trumpet is going to toot and we're going to scoot! It's not the past or future part that many believers have a problem with, it's the believing for today part that causes them to struggle. While Christianity is a miracle faith, it is often easier to believe that Jesus performed great miracles in the past or that the miracle of eternity is waiting— but that a miracle will happen right in the middle of our current circumstances can be difficult to believe in full faith.

Whether we truly believe in the possibility of miracles today or not, Jesus was quite clear in John 14:12 when He said, "I tell you the truth, anyone who believes in me will do the same works I have done, and even greater works, because I am going to be with the Father." He didn't say certain people, He said *anyone*. He didn't say similar or great, He said *same and greater*. Jesus went on to explain that He was going to be with the Father so the Holy Spirit could come. The key to not only seeing the same and greater works but being used to accomplish the same and greater works is the power of the Holy Spirit living within us.

WHAT GREATER LOOKS LIKE

Christians are not exempt from doubt, we all experience feelings of doubt in different moments or even seasons of life. Doubt is not the opposite of faith; unbelief is the opposite of faith. Jesus said in Luke 7:28 that "of all who have ever lived, none is greater than John."

Although John the Baptist was greater than anyone who had ever lived, he struggled with doubt. In Matthew 11 he was thrown in prison and was hearing of all the great things Jesus was doing – all the great things except getting him out of jail. He began to doubt if Jesus was really the Messiah.

Upon hearing of John the Baptist's doubt, Jesus told His disciples in Matthew 11:4-5, "Go back to John and tell him what you have heard and seen—the blind see, the lame walk, those with leprosy are cured, the deaf hear, the dead are raised to life, and the Good News is being preached to the poor." The physical miracles of healing were mentioned first, but Jesus saved the most important miracle for last—the Good News was preached. Jesus was saying that no matter how great of a miracle God performs to heal or provide for a person here on earth, they will still die. The greatest miracle happens when a person hears the gospel and gives their life to Christ. Jesus wasn't simply performing miracles to bring healing; He was offering salvation because He was the Messiah—the only One who can save. Always remember that there is something far greater than being healed, that's being made whole!

To understand what Jesus meant by believers being able to do "even greater" works, you can't get confused by thinking that "even greater" means bigger or better. Notice that miracles in the Bible always happen in proximity to God's presence. The disciples were in close proximity to Jesus when miracles were performed. Jesus knew that when He went to be with the Father, miracles on earth wouldn't be possible without closeness to the Presence of God. But He knew that the Holy Spirit would come to live inside every believer, which allowed God's presence to spread to every corner of the earth and the gospel to be preached to all people in every way possible. "Even greater" doesn't mean bigger or better; it means more numerous.

THE MIRACULOUS PURPOSE

Miracles don't simply happen to draw crowds or impress people. There is an eternal purpose tied to every miracle. In Biblical times, miracles were performed for three purposes: authentication, revelation, and glorification.

Miracles are often referred to as signs that point to or indicate something. That reminds me of a story I heard about a husband and wife who were driving down a road and saw a sign that read Road Closed. The husband ignored the sign and kept driving. The wife said, "Honey, you need to turn around because the road is closed. Didn't you see the sign?" The husband did not care what the sign said, he was adamant that they would be fine to continue in the direction they were going.

After driving another mile or so, they came to a barrier in the road and a large sign with the words BRIDGE OUT in bold orange letters. The wife said, "See, I told you that sign was correct. The road is closed because the bridge is out. Now you definitely have to turn around and go all the way back!" The husband finally agreed, and as drove back down the road, he passed the first sign and noticed that the back of the sign read Welcome Back, Stupid!

Signs are purposefully placed to provide needed direction or to indicate necessary information. In the same way that many signs are placed in precise locations because the information on them can be vitally important to people, the signs and miracles that Jesus performed in the Bible were vitally important to those receiving and those witnessing the miracle.

Many of the miracles that were performed in Jesus' day provided authentication of what He said and who He was. In Mark 2 four men brought their friend to Jesus for healing but couldn't get into the house. They believed in Jesus' ability to heal so much that they tore the roof off of the house and lowered their friend through the ceiling. Jesus saw their faith and said, "My child, your sins are forgiven" (v. 5). Of course, the religious teachers were appalled by Jesus' statement because they didn't believe Him to be the Messiah sent by God.

Jesus knew the thoughts of unbelief that were going through the religious teachers' heads, so He performed a miracle to authenticate His Words and His authority to forgive sins. In Mark 2:10–11, He addressed those who didn't believe saying, "Is it easier to say to the paralyzed man, 'Your sins are forgiven,' or 'Stand up, pick up your mat, and walk'? So I will prove to you that the Son of Man has the authority on earth to forgive sins." Then Jesus turned to the paralyzed man and said, "Stand up, pick up your mat, and go home!" The purpose in His miracle went far beyond that of restoring a man's mobility, it pointed to the Messiah.

Revelation was also a purpose of miracles in Jesus' day. Miracles were performed to reveal the kingdom of God to people on earth. In Matthew 28, Jesus cast out a demon from a man so that he could speak and see once again. The Pharisees did not like that people were beginning to believe that Jesus was the Messiah, so they claimed that He could only cast out devils because "He gets his power from Satan" (v. 24).

Jesus uses this opportunity to not only discredit the Pharisees but provide revelation. In Matthew 12:27–28, Jesus says, "And if I am empowered by Satan, what about your own exorcists? They cast out demons, too, so they will condemn you for what you have said. But if I am casting out demons by the Spirit of God, then the Kingdom of God has arrived among you." Why did Jesus cast out devils? To prove that the kingdom of God had come and that the God of the kingdom had come!

Miracles were also performed to provide glorification of God. In Mark 2, after Jesus healed the man to prove that He was the One who could forgive sins, the man jumped up, grabbed his mat, and left the house. Verse 12 says that those who witnessed the miracle were in shock: "They were all amazed and praised God, exclaiming, 'We've never seen anything like this before!'" The result of the miracle was not only the man's forgiveness but the room full of spectators began to give God glory for all that had been done!

You may think biblical miracles aren't seen as much today, and I would say that is because the purpose for miracles today is glorification. You see, when Jesus was speaking to and teaching the people He encountered, they didn't have a complete Bible to authenticate what He was saying. They couldn't look back through God's Word to verify if

> *We need to make sure that every miracle brings glory and honor to God above all else.*

what He was saying aligned with God. They also didn't have complete scripture that provides a full revelation of God's plan for His kingdom here on Earth. But we have a complete Bible. We can study His Word for authentication and revelation, so miracles today are meant to bring glory to God. So we need to make sure that every miracle brings glory and honor to God above all else.

STOP LOOKING AND START LETTING

Many Christians spend their entire lives waiting for God to show them a great miracle or to work miracles in their lives. Some people want a "water into wine" situation or a "walking on water" experience. I'm not saying those things can't happen—God can do anything, but those people will most likely be disappointed in their waiting. God wants to do more than show you great things.

Maybe you are that person waiting for a biblical-style miracle to happen in your life. While you're waiting for God to work a miracle, He's waiting for you to let the Holy Spirit work through you to make miracles happen. Spectators stand on the sidelines and watch, but that's not what you were created or called to do. We all are meant to operate as the hands and feet of Jesus.

James 1:22 teaches us, "Don't just listen to God's word. You must do what it says. Otherwise, you are only fooling yourselves." And nowhere in the Bible does it tell us to get saved and then just sit back and wait for heaven.

The Bible makes it clear in Ephesians 2:8 that it is "by grace you have been saved through faith. And this is not your own doing; it is the gift of God, not a result of works," but that's not to say God doesn't expect us to do anything after our salvation. In fact, James 2 mentions many times that faith with no actions to back it up is dead and useless. Paul urges believers to allow their bodies to "be a living and holy sacrifice," which means we allow the Holy Spirit to work in and through us for the kingdom of God.

While you're waiting for God to work a miracle, He's waiting for you to let the Holy Spirit work through you to make miracles happen.

You may want to see God resurrect a person from physical death, but God wants to use your life to resurrect people from spiritual death. Through you, He can work to bring others from sin and salvation. If you will surrender completely to the Holy Spirit and become a vehicle with which He brings about miracles, He will use you to perform resurrections from fear to faith, from shameful to courageous, from addiction to freedom, from victim to victor, and so much more!

Don't get so busy looking for God to show up in a social media-worthy moment that you miss out on the Holy Spirit using you in a sinner-made-worthy miracle! It's time to stop being a sideline spectator and start allowing the Holy Spirit access to your time, talents, and treasure to do the miraculous works for which you were created! The time is now for you to surrender to the power and presence of the Holy Spirit who will help prepare you for greatness and develop holy expectation.

PREPARE FOR GREATNESS

Regardless of where you are in your walk with Christ or how long you've been a Christian, you can begin preparing today for the Holy Spirit to perform miraculous works in and through your life. John Bevere once said that "spiritual maturity is tied to obedience, not time." It's not about how long you've known the Lord but how long you've been fully surrendered to the Lord and obedient to His calling on your life.

I remember as a young kid I watched the United States hockey team play the Soviet Union for the gold medal during the 1980 Winter Olympics. Everyone was certain that the Soviet Union team would win because they had won four out of the past five gold medals and all of their players were seasoned veterans on the ice. It didn't help that team USA was the youngest team in the tournament and was made up of all amateur players. That fact alone shouldn't have worried anyone much, because after all, amateurs built the ark and professionals built the Titanic.

Though no one expected the young, inexperienced United States team to win, they came out on top with a 4-3 upset over the defending gold medalists! That game became an iconic event in Olympic Games history and has since been referred to as the Miracle on Ice.

While I wouldn't call the win a miracle, I do think that monumental game relates in a lot of ways to our walk with Christ. Those young team members were not considered the most qualified players individually, but their win proved that when you are on the right team and in the right position, miracles can happen. When you are on God's team and you let the Holy Spirit guide you to the right position, you will be prepared to participate with God in great and miraculous works!

Preparation for and participation in kingdom work looks a lot different than how to world would prepare for something wonderful. When it comes to miraculous works, don't plan to attract people but to attract God's presence. It should never be about drawing a crowd as much as it should be about drawing Christ. Attracting the Holy Spirit should always take priority over obtaining a higher status.

God will ask for your obedience in private long before anything happens in public.

Kingdom work will always require more private preparation than public performance. A.W. Tozer once said, "Any tiny work that God has ever done through me and through my ministry for Him dates back to that hour when I was filled with the Spirit." Fresh fillings of the Holy Spirit daily are vital to God using your life to impact others for eternity. Gratitude and obedience are key elements of private preparation.

The Bible is clear that Jesus prioritized alone time with God and expressed gratitude before performing great miracles. In both accounts of Jesus feeding a multitude of people with a few loaves of bread and a few fish in Matthew 14 and 15, He blessed the food and thanked God for it before performing the miracle of feeding thousands. Then, in John 11, Jesus raised Lazarus from the dead. Before calling Lazarus forth, Jesus looked to heaven and thanked God for hearing Him. Gratitude is a magnet for miracles!

Preparing for greatness will always require obedience, and God will ask for your obedience in private long before anything happens in public. When you work to maintain a close relationship with the Holy Spirit, you will be aware of His voice prompting you to follow where He leads, and the more you hear Him and become confident in recognizing His voice above all other noise, the easier it will be to obey. I encourage you to dedicate yourself to closeness with the Holy Spirit. Prioritize spiritual disciple and prepare to be used greatly. God comes to prepared places, and I pray that you are preparing your heart and your life for miraculous works. God has very specific ways in which He wants you to use your life and your gifts as you walk in your calling!

HOLY EXPECTATION

If you long for God to use your life for kingdom work, you must maintain an eternal perspective and have holy expectations. I've often said that a lot of people have let their expect or expire. You must not only believe that God can perform miraculous works, but you must expect that He will.

When you understand the incredible power you have within you because of the presence of the Holy Spirit, you will have a holy expectation for God to do something miraculous in your daily life. Because the Holy Spirit lives inside of me, I expect the Holy Spirit to lead me into holy moments in which miraculous things *will* happen. I learned to expect the unexplainable because that's when God receives all the glory.

As I've said before, our church has experienced tremendous growth over the past thirty years. Most of what has happened in and around our church is beyond any earthly explanation. Not long after taking the job as the senior pastor of Rock Springs Church, I sat down with a man in the church to go over my ten-year plan. I remember him looking at me like I was crazy, but I just knew that God would exceed anything I could imagine, so why not make big plans.

I knew early on that one of our biggest struggles would be acquiring enough land because God was going to grow our church and we would need room to build. There were one hundred acres across the street from the church, and I started praying for the Lord to give us that land. Over the course of thirty years, I inquired about the church buying the land over and over, but will every offer, I was told that they would never sell it. But I kept praying because I expected God to make it happen.

After more than thirty years of praying, God gave us that land in 2022. It was a miracle that the landowner agreed to sell, but even beyond the accepted offer, God provided the funds to secure the purchase. A man came to me and said that if the church raised the first half of the money, he would give the second half. Our people were so faithful to give because they knew their money was supporting a miracle. They too had been praying for many years. After all the preparation behind the scenes, they were eager to let the Holy Spirit use them to bring it all to fruition.

Maintaining a holy expectation may seem easier said than done. Even Peter had a hard time believing God for a miracle after being thrown in prison by King Herod Agrippa. In Acts 12, Peter was awaiting execution and didn't expect God to rescue Him, so he went to sleep. Even when an angel came to lead him out of the prison to safety, he thought it was merely a dream.

When he realized he was truly free, he went to Mary's house where people were praying that God would rescue Peter from execution. But when the servant told everyone that Peter was knocking on the door, they didn't believe her, they thought it must be his ghost.

I hope that you will not only pray that God will do miraculous works in and through your life but that you will truly believe He can and expect that He will. Don't be like Peter and his friends who prayed for God to move but then doubted the miracle. Pray for it, expect it, recognize it, and immediately give God glory for it!

I sincerely pray that you would come to know the Holy Spirit on such a deep level that you trust Him with every aspect of your life and believe with the holy expectation that He will do infinitely more than you could ever imagine or plan for yourself.

Your life, in and of itself, is a miracle because your Creator has always been in the miracle-working business. Just as you are a miracle, you were created for miracles, and there are miracle opportunities all around you every day. You just need the divine understanding and guidance of the Holy Spirit to reveal them to you. Allow Him to prepare you, lead you, and use you for the kingdom purpose that you were created to fulfill through the unique calling He's placed on your life. You'll never regret being obedient to the Holy Spirit's prompting to participate in miraculous works!

TIME TO REFLECT

- What comfort do you take in knowing that God doesn't change? Is there anything about that fact that you don't like? Have you ever wished that there were certain things about God that would change? If yes, in what ways have you wanted Him to change or possibly be different?

- Have you ever been reluctant to give God the glory for something amazing in your life?

- How might your life being used by God for miraculous works make you uncomfortable? Are there social pressures that make it difficult or uncomfortable to glorify God when miracles happen?

- Do you struggle with maintaining holy expectation? In what ways have you prayed for certain things in your life without having a holy expectation of God moving or working? What can you do today that would help you maintain holy expectation?

CONCLUSION
UNLIMITED LIVING

I BEGAN THIS BOOK by telling you that preaching a six-week sermon series on the Holy Spirit brought about a transformation in my life and my ministry. As church staff, we have all been in agreement that the trajectory of our church changed because of that series, but we had never really shared much about the specific, personal ways in which transformation occurred in individual lives. When I started writing this book, more of my conversations with my staff naturally turned toward how the Holy Spirit has worked in a mighty way over the years.

We have often discussed how much our services have changed since 2016. Our staff no longer plans and prepares for services with personal preferences in mind or with the goal of getting people interested in what we're doing. Once everyone came to the understanding of the vital role the Holy Spirit has in the success of a service, our number one focus has been planning and preparing everything in such a way that attracts the presence of the Holy Spirit. Because if the Holy Spirit comes, people can't help but be interested and transformation will be inevitable.

Several of my staff members began to share their personal stories, and I've been blown away by just how good God has been to work in and through people who place a priority on a deep relationship with the Holy Spirit. Most staff members began to share about their upbringing, and while several of them have stories a lot like mine where church was a foreign concept in their homes growing up, many of them said they grew up faithfully attending their churches without ever learning about the Holy Spirit. Because of certain denominational beliefs, the Holy Spirit wasn't validated or ever mentioned in some of their church experiences. I don't know that one single staff member expressed having confidence in their knowledge and relationship with the Holy Spirit prior to 2016.

That left me eager to know specific details of how things have changed in their personal lives since prioritizing the Holy Spirit in their daily walk. The biggest change that most people shared was the awareness of His voice prompting them to recognize "God moments" throughout their day. Not just in their ministry experiences but in their home lives. The Holy Spirit has worked to strengthen and even restore marriages that were struggling and on the brink of divorce. Because parents relied on the Holy Spirit to lead and guide their homes, the communication within their home has been transformed. There is more grace, compassion, and patience.

The confidence in their knowledge of the Holy Spirit left many of them with a desire to invite Him into every area of their lives and ministries. They have developed a passion for sharing their knowledge of all that He can do with others. It's as if deep love of the Holy Spirit has become contagious and people are desperate to share Him with whoever they can!

Now let me hasten to say that all has not been sunshine and rainbows since 2016. Many within our church and even on our staff have walked through some incredibly dark circumstances. As a staff, we've relied on the Holy Spirit to provide strength that only comes from Him as individuals have experienced incredible heartache through the loss of loved ones, tragic accidents that left them weary on the road to recovery, battles with anxiety and depression, crippling stress and fear that comes from raising children in a fallen world, among many other situations.

Though we've seen our fair share of difficulty, relying on the presence and power of the Holy Spirit is the only reason that any of us has made it through each and every trial. The Holy Spirit has a way of reminding us of truth in just the right moments. He has always given us the right perspective to realize that our battles are not flesh and blood but spiritual. Even in difficulty, He has been so faithful to lead us and sustain us in our calling. God has been so good to provide, not in all the ways that we wanted but in all the ways we've needed.

I hope you know that our entire staff has been praying ahead of this book with a holy expectation that God is going to transform *your* life through the work of the Holy Spirit. We know first-hand what happens when the Holy Spirit becomes the priority. We know the pressure that gets lifted when you allow Him to have complete access to and control over every aspect of your life. The Christian life won't always be easy but it will always be good and worth every moment if you allow the Holy Spirit to provide your every need.

I encourage you to seek the Holy Spirit like you never have before. Give Him your all. Let your life be an outward witness of the Holy Spirit within you. Maybe you began reading this book with absolutely no knowledge of the Holy Spirit, maybe you had some preconceived ideas of Who He is, or maybe you knew Him but have never pursued closeness with Him. If your perspective has been too narrow, your expectations too low, and your dreams too small, I pray that this book has given you an eternal perspective, holy expectation, and a desire to trust the Lord for great and mighty things in your own life and the lives of those around you. With the presence and power of the Holy Spirit dwelling within you daily, the possibilities are endless and your potential is unlimited!

Dear heavenly Father, I thank You for Your unfailing love for us. You have never failed to provide for our every need. Thank You for the gift of salvation through Your Son, Jesus Christ. You love us so much and desire closeness with us that exceeds any earthly connection we could ever have. Thank You for sending the Holy Spirit to dwell within us so that we may experience the perfect peace that comes only in Your presence. Helps us each day to know You better and make You known through the divine wisdom we have through Your Spirit. Lead us in our unique purpose as we surrender to You each day. May You receive all glory, honor, and praise for all that is accomplished in Your Name through our lives. Have Your will and way today and forever. In Jesus' precious name I pray, amen.

APPENDIX

PRAYER OF SALVATION

I<small>F YOU WANT</small> to ask Jesus into your heart and spend eternity with Him in heaven, salvation is as easy as ABC!

- Acknowledge that you are a sinner.
- Believe that Jesus died on the cross for your sins.
- Confess your sins to Him.

Pray this prayer with me:

Lord Jesus, I am a sinner and I am sorry for my sins. I'm so sorry that I want to change. I believe You died on the cross as payment for my sins. I confess my sins to You right now. Come into my heart, Lord. Come into my life and forgive me. Thank You, Jesus, for forgiving me. Thank You for saving me!

If you prayed that prayer, I encourage you to tell someone about the decision you have made. I hope you will reach out to others to help you in your new walk with the Lord! I hope you will get plugged in to a local church and continue to grow in your relationship with God!

If you know someone who doesn't know Jesus as their Lord

and Savior, I pray that you will have an opportunity to share the gospel with them. I hope you are able to use the prayer above to lead others in praying the prayer of salvation.

SPIRITUAL GIFTS TEST

If you are interested in learning more about your spiritual gifts, use the links below to take a free spiritual gifts test online. Once you identify your spiritual gifts, I encourage you to continue learning more about your gifts and seek ways in which you can use your gifts. If you are not already involved in a local church, I encourage you to get involved and seek ways to serve within the church using your spiritual gifts! Visit www.giftstest.com or www.spiritualgiftstest.com.

NOTES

FOREWORD

1. "Apostles' Creed," Christian Reformed Church, accessed July 24, 2023, https://www.crcna.org/welcome/beliefs/creeds/apostles-creed.

INTRODUCTION

1. "Oswald Chambers," AZ Quotes, accessed July 25, 2023, https://www.azquotes.com/quote/827729.

CHAPTER 1

1. Mayo Clinic staff, "Dehydration: Overview," Mayo Clinic, October 14, 2021, https://www.mayoclinic.org/diseases-conditions/dehydration/symptoms-causes/syc-20354086.
2. Dr. George Barna, "American Worldview Inventory 2021," Cultural Research Center, Arizona Christian University, August 31, 2021, https://www.arizonachristian.edu/wp-content/uploads/2021/08/CRC_AWVI2021_Release06_Digital_01_20210831.pdf.
3. "Augustine of Hippo," Goodreads, accessed July 26, 2023, https://www.goodreads.com/about/us.
4. Jack Hyles, "Praying for Laborers," in *Exploring Prayer With Jack Hyles* (Hammond, IN: Hyles-Anderson Publishers, 1983), chapter 35.

CHAPTER 2

1. Blue Letter Bible, s.v. "*ginōskō*," accessed July 27, 2023, https://www.blueletterbible.org/lexicon/g1097/kjv/tr/0-1/.

CHAPTER 3

1. "Billy Sunday," Goodreads, accessed August 14, 2023, https://www.goodreads.com/quotes/190658-the-only-way-to-keep-a-broken-vessel-full-is.
2. "Dwight L. Mooody," Goodreads, accessed July 27, 2023, https://www.goodreads.com/quotes/4474-i-firmly-believe-that-the-moment-our-hearts-are-emptied.
3. "A. W. Tozer," Goodreads, accessed July 27, 2023, https://www.goodreads.com/author/quotes/1082290.A_W_Tozer?page=57.

CHAPTER 4

1. Andrew Murray, *The Indwelling Spirit: The Work of the Holy Spirit in the Life of the Believer* (Ada, MI: Baker Books, 2006), 9.
2. Blue Letter Bible, s.v. "*oikeō*," accessed July 31, 2023, https://www.blueletterbible.org/lexicon/g3611/nasb20/tr/0-1/.
3. Blue Letter Bible, s.v. "*paraklētos*," accessed July 31, 2023, https://www.blueletterbible.org/lexicon/g3875/kjv/tr/0-1/.

4. "The Father Who Helped His Son Cross the Finish Line at the Olympics Has Died," NPR, October 4, 2022, https://www.npr.org/2022/10/04/1126776697/jim-redmond-derek-olympics-sprinter-father-dies#:~:text=via%20Getty%20Images-,British%20runner%20Derek%20Redmond%20limps%20around%20the%20track%20toward%20the,this%20week%20at%20age%2081.

5. "Top 10 W. Ian Thomas Quotes (2023 Update)," Quotefancy, accessed August 5, 2023, https://quotefancy.com/w-ian-thomas-quotes.

CHAPTER 5

1. "What Is Sociology?," American Sociological Association, accessed July 31, 2023, https://www.asanet.org/about/what-sociology.

2. "Quotes of Hudson Taylor," Prevailing Intercessory Prayer, accessed August 5, 2023, https://www.path2prayer.com/famous-christians-their-lives-and-writings-including-free-books/j-hudson-taylor-pioneer-missionary-to-china/quotes-of-hudson-taylor.

3. "Abraham Lincoln," Goodreads, accessed August 1, 2023, https://www.goodreads.com/quotes/9938-whatever-you-are-be-a-good-one

4. Blue Letter Bible, s.v. *"agathōsynē,"* accessed July 31, 2023, https://www.blueletterbible.org/lexicon/g19/nasb20/tr/0-1/.

CHAPTER 6

1. Blue Letter Bible, s.v. "rule," accessed August 15, 2023, https://www.blueletterbible.org/search/Dictionary/viewTopic.cfm?topic=VT0002442.

2. Eric Suni, "Dreams," Sleep Foundation, updated August 1, 2023, https://www.sleepfoundation.org/dreams.

3. *Merriam-Webster*, s.v. "fellowship," accessed August 14, 2023, https://www.merriam-webster.com/dictionary/fellowship

CHAPTER 7

1. Blue Letter Bible, s.v. *"thyō,"* accessed August 15, 2023, https://www.blueletterbible.org/lexicon/g2380/kjv/tr/0-1/.

2. Jim Cymbala, *Spiritual Warfare Is Real* (Nashville, TN: HarperChristian Resources, 2021).

3. A. W. Tozer, *The Quotable Tozer: A Topical Compilation of the Wisdom and Insight of A. W. Tozer* (Ada, MI: Baker Books, 2018).

CHAPTER 8

1. "Max Lucado," AZ Quotes, accessed August 22, 2023, https://www.azquotes.com/quote/568754.

CHAPTER 10

1. Blue Letter Bible, s.v. *"poiēma,"* accessed July 31, 2023, https://www.blueletterbible.org/lexicon/g4161/nlt/mgnt/0-1/.